WHAT WERE THEY THINKING?

WHAT WERE THEY THINKING?

The Brainless Blunders That Changed Sports History

KYLE GARLETT

Author of THE WORST CALL EVER!

HARPER

An Imprint of HarperCollinsPublishers

HarperCollins books may be purchased for educational, business, or sales promotional use. For information, please write: Special Markets Department, HarperCollins Publishers, 10 East 53rd Street, New York, NY 10022.

FIRST EDITION

Designed by William Ruoto

Library of Congress Cataloging-in-Publication Data

Garlett, Kyle.
What were they thinking? : the brainless blunders that changed sports history / Kyle Garlett.—1st ed.
p. cm.
ISBN 978-0-06-169992-4
1. Sports—History—Miscellanea. I. Title.
GV707.G37 2009
796.09—dc22
2008045112

09 10 11 12 13 OV/RRD 10 9 8 7 6 5 4 3 2 1

For the fan. You suffer among friends.

CONTENTS

ACKNOWLEDGMENTS

First and foremost I have to thank Timmy Jenkins of Wichita, Kansas. It was you, back when I was a Little League umpire in the summer of 1986, who first planted the seeds of written comedy in sports buffoonery when I watched you lose the Six-Years-Old-and-Under baseball championship by running to the wrong base in the 5th inning. You cried that day . . . and probably several since. But thank you.

I would be remiss if I didn't mention the following giants in sports embarrassment that have contributed mightily to the subject at hand: College football coach Gary Barnett, pioneer of the stripper- and escort-attended recruitment parties (allegedly). French soccer coach Raymond Domenech, who refused to play anyone born under the astrological sign Scorpio (seriously). High school cross-country coach Brenton Wuchae, who at the age of forty married one of his sixteen-year-old athletes. And Austrian ski coach Walter Mayer, who, after fleeing the Torino Olympics following a raid that uncovered numerous syringes and a blood transfusion machine, crashed his car into a police roadblock.

Let us all be inspired by your commitment to stupidity.

Finally, I must thank the many athletes who, through their

daily actions both on and off the field, gave me an avalanche of material to sift through. And a specific thank-you to basketball great Patrick Ewing, who provided the inspirational quote that I have attached to my computer monitor and that always kept me focused on the task at hand. During the 1998–99 NBA lockout, when explaining the need for a charity basketball game to raise money for out-of-work players, Ewing said, "Sure, we make a lot of money. But we spend a lot of money, too."

Without you, the following pages would not be possible.

INTRODUCTION

The history of our world has been shaped by the kaleidoscope of mistakes human beings have made. Do a Google search of the word "mistake" and you get roughly 121 million results, give or take. Mistakes, in all forms, so permeate the multiple facets of our lives that we have created literally dozens of other words that mean "mistake."

You've got your blunders, bloopers, bloomers, balks, boners, bobbles, and bungles, and that's just the Bs. Never mind the miscues, missteps, misconceptions, miscalculations, and misunderstandings.

Writer James Joyce said, "Mistakes are the portals of discovery."

But Albert Einstein said, "Only two things are infinite, the universe and human stupidity, and I'm not sure about the former."

And that would explain why, even though we've now opened up roughly 121 million of Joyce's "portals of discovery," we continue to make, repeat, and repeat yet again the original errors.

If author John Powell was right when he said, "The only real mistake is the one from which we learn nothing," then we are a society of idiots awash in our ignorance. And, of course, the sports world is far from immune. In fact, it might best be described as an overgrown forest of fools beyond a pruner's relieving shears.

We've all heard about that one poor sap in our office who accidentally hit "reply all" when his overly personal e-mail was meant for only one set of understanding eyes. And we've all laughed a little at his embarrassment, as long as his workplace punishment didn't go beyond the requisite ridicule from coworkers.

But have you heard about the case of Steelers line coach Larry Zierlein? As probably happens from time to time with a professional sports organization that has access to the Internet, Zierlein sent out an e-mail that had a pornographic video attached to it. But what doesn't usually happen, and what makes Zierlein's e-mail noteworthy in the vast sea of adult-oriented online exchanges, is that Zierlein accidentally sent the video to a large list of league recipients that included all thirty-two team general managers, their secretaries, and NFL commissioner Roger Goodell.

Zierlein kept his job but suffered more humiliation than any Southwest Airlines "Want to Get Away" commercial could possibly portray. "It's hard because I made an inexcusable mistake," Zierlein said. "It was hard first for the organization. They had to explain and go through . . . and my family, for what they're going to have to hear."

Let Zierlein's pain be your cautionary tale.

We've all at some point knocked our heads against an open cabinet, slammed our fingers in some sort of closing door, and stubbed our toe because even though we've stepped through it a thousand times before, we forgot this once about the small half-step up in our kitchen's entryway. But none of those everyday, painfully humbling mishaps compare to what kicker Bill Gramatica did as a rookie in 2001. Celebrating a meaningless 42-yard first-quarter field goal for the not-going-anywhere Arizona

Cardinals, Gramatica began hopping around like his feet were on fire.

This was Gramatica's standard celebration following kicks of any length or importance, including extra points. But what wasn't standard, and what made Gramatica a laughingstock and secured him a permanent place on the all-time dumbest sports injuries list, was the torn ACL that his hopping resulted in, ending his season.

And we've all, at least once, been late in meeting a boss's or teacher's deadline on a work or school assignment. But it's also probably safe to say that afterward we weren't raked over the coals for it by the local and national media, as were the Minnesota Vikings when in 2003 they were late in making their first-round draft pick. The Vikings had the seventh pick in that April's draft, but by letting the clock run out on them before submitting their selection to league officials, they didn't actually pick until ninth.

When, at every yearly NFL draft, the commissioner says, "[insert team name here] is on the clock," between each and every pick, it's best to take that clock seriously.

These mistakes and errors in judgment driven by Einstein's theory of infinite human stupidity are mere drops in a bottomless bucket that overflows with unadulterated moronity. And in truth, at the end of the day in these few examples here, there was very little collateral damage. The parties injured by these wrong turns in reason were contained to the small group of offenders.

But, of course, lapses in brain function are not always benign. For every ill-advised interoffice e-mail deleted and then forgotten, and for each self-inflicted knee injury that fails to make a difference in the season's final standings, there are dim-witted decisions of considerable consequence. Moves made or not made, things said and done, and blunders in strategy that have at times altered the course of sports history in dramatic and meaningful ways.

Very few vocations are as committed to keeping the record of past triumphs and failures as is the world of sports. *The Baseball Encyclopedia* chronicles every single at bat taken throughout the history of baseball—the home runs and the strikeouts. *Pro Football Weekly* keeps track of every win and loss, touchdown and turnover, and eventual Super Bowl champion. And if you have a basketball question involving a player, stat, or game result, *InsideHoops* is the place to go.

But when it comes to errors of the mind, decisions absurdly divergent from practices that are tried and true, and regrettable words and actions that will forever haunt the men and women who made them, the history books are noticeably quiet.

Not anymore.

Let this volume stand as the incomplete, and completely decided upon by no one other than the author, historical record of all things in sports that are stupid and senseless. If it was brainless, irrational, or otherwise imbecilic, and it ultimately influenced sports history's final transcript, it's in this book. Or I simply didn't have room to include it, and you can read about in Volume II.

Or Volume III.

Because if there is one thing more dependable than the ocean tides, rising sun, and shoddy mothering of Dina Lohan, it's the constant conveyor belt of human idiocy.

COACHES/
MANAGERS

In the history of the National Football League—which extends officially back to the NFL's creation in 1920 at a car dealership in Canton, Ohio—nearly three hundred men have at one time roamed the sidelines carrying the title of head coach. Yet as of the induction ceremonies in Canton, Ohio, in 2008, only twenty-one of these leaders of men have been honored with enshrinement into the Pro Football Hall of Fame.

Depending on what source you look at, there have been in the neighborhood of 650 different men who at one time have been managers in Major League Baseball. As debasing as it may be to admit when talking about America's national pastime, according to Bill "Mr. Baseball Britannica" James, the first of these "managers" (at the time a combination of team captain and business manager) was an Englishman and professional cricket player named Harry Wright. He got the job with the Boston Red Stockings in 1871 after his younger brother George—at the time considered baseball's best player—turned it down.

But when Dick Williams was inducted into Cooperstown in 2008 he was just the nineteenth field manager in history to gain membership to the Hall. Out of the nearly one thousand men who have been a head coach or manager in one of our nation's two biggest sports, only forty have been considered good enough for their sport's highest honor. You have to think that if these Hall of Famers would have coached in today's era of instant "win today or gone tomorrow" gratification, many of them would have ended up on the scrap heap of unrealized fan expectations.

Before Hall of Famer Chuck Noll won four Super Bowls in Pittsburgh, he finished 1-13 as a first-year head coach and won just 12 games in his first three seasons. And we know Miller Huggins as the manager of those great Yankees teams in the 1920s. But before making it to New York, and the Hall of Fame, Huggins managed the Cardinals for five seasons, losing 69 more games than he won. (Of course, he didn't have Babe Ruth and Lou Gehrig with him in St. Louis.)

So, what do these numbers mean? Have we been saddled with a mass of mediocre managers and coaches through the years? Or are we overflowing with greatness, but unable to recognize it because today coaches are given about six weeks to win, or else.

I don't know. But I do know that no matter how intelligent, decisive, skilled, and experienced coaches or managers may be, they will always make some decisions that leave us questioning their sanity. And that goes well beyond the presently unexplained choice by baseball to have its well-past-playing-shape field managers and coaches squeezing into form-fitting baseball pants. (Is there some overlooked provision in the rules that would allow Lou Piniella to insert himself into the lineup in the event that he found himself short on outfielders?)

The need for a Tim Gunn fashion makeover and the installation of a full-length mirror in every manager's personal office notwithstanding, the sanity-questioning moves that I'm talking about were history-changing—and egregious enough to warrant each of the following eighteen nominees your consideration for the Coaches and Managers Hall of Infamy.

An inconsolable Ralph Branca sits on the Dodgers' clubhouse steps after giving up the home run to Bobby Thomson that won the 1951 National League pennant for the Giants. Branca never should have been in the game, but manager Charlie Dressen unwisely thought otherwise. *(Rogers Photo Archive/Getty Images)*

Shot Heard 'Round the World

October 3, 1951—National League Tiebreaker Game 3,
Dodgers vs. Giants

You can no doubt trace our love of the home run directly back to our primordial respect for all things strong and powerful. It's in our DNA. How else can you explain the $16 million that Sylvester Stallone's 1987 arm-wrestling yarn *Over the Top* made at the domestic box office? Or why when I'm flipping through my 167 channels of sports programming (God bless DirecTV) and I come across guys throwing kegs, carrying refrigerators, and pulling boxcars on reruns of *The World's Strongest Man*, I'm forced to cancel the rest of my day's appointments so I can marvel at Iceland's Magnus Ver Magnusson gripping the Pillars of Hercules.

If the Mighty Casey had been a slap singles hitter with great speed, Mudvillians would have gotten over their joyless afternoon by dinnertime. And does anyone really care, or even know, that in his career Babe Ruth hit more than twice as many triples as Rickey Henderson?

In baseball, the home run is king. Among the most celebrated of America's most famous dingers, none can compare in acclaim or account to the Shot Heard 'Round the World that divided the boroughs of the city of New York and sent the Giants on to the 1951 World Series.

You may remember the home run hit on April 8, 1974, that lifted Hank Aaron past Babe Ruth on the all-time home-run list with 715. But so much more than one hit defines the career of the twenty-four-time All-Star. You've probably seen the replays of Roger Maris's 61 in '61 that broke Ruth's thirty-four-year-old single-season home-run record. But with two MVP awards and World Series rings won in both leagues, one record (since broken) was hardly Maris's greatest baseball accomplishment.

For Bobby Thomson, however, the story's different. His pennant-winning home run in 1951 not only made the slightly above-average outfielder a household name more than fifty years after his retirement; it resulted in the same baseball immortality for the other players involved—most notably the man who served up the notorious gopher ball, Dodgers pitcher Ralph Branca. Although if it hadn't been for the grudge held by Brooklyn manager Charlie Dressen toward pitcher Clem Labine, the historical home run would have likely never happened.

The 1951 season should have never come down to a playoff

between the Brooklyn Dodgers and New York Giants. Brooklyn spent a total of 120 days that season in first place. And it led the National League by as many as 13 games as late as August 11. As Dressen said numerous times that season, including during an early April locker room sing-along after the Dodgers took five straight games from the crosstown league rivals, sending the Giants to a disastrous season-opening 2-12 start, "Roll out the barrel, the Giants are dead!" Although, as it turned out, the mid-season reports of their death were greatly exaggerated.

Starting on August 12 with a doubleheader sweep of the Phillies, the Giants won an incredible 16 games in a row, playing .840 baseball (37-7) over their final 44 games. Meanwhile, over that same 44-game period, the Dodgers scuffled their way to a 24-20 record, securing their heartbreaking place in history by surrendering the biggest August lead of all time—a record collapse that to this day remains unmatched.

Much has been made of the allegations that the Giants and manager Leo Durocher spent the second half of the 1951 season—armed with a telescoped center-field lookout and elaborate buzzer system—stealing signs. And thus, stealing wins by cheating. But because impartiality demands that baseball's paragon of comeback stories receive more commendation than confrontation, it should be noted that during its closing sprint to the finish, New York was 17-4 on the road—away from the purposefully partisan Polo Grounds.

Of course, had the Dodgers won just one more game during the final two months of the season, none of these details would have been remembered, or been relevant, beyond the waning days of that October.

In August, with the Dodgers pitching staff becoming decimated by injury and fatigued by overuse, the team handed the ball to the twenty-four-year-old arm of Clem Labine—a talented and gritty player who spent the final two years of World War II as a paratrooper. In his first career start, on August 28, Labine handled the Reds, 3–1. He then beat the Braves, 7–2; the Reds again, 7–0; and the Cubs, 6–1—running his record to 4-0 with hardly a hint of adversity. It looked like Labine, who would finish third in Rookie of the Year voting that year (Willie Mays won the award), was just what the Dodgers ordered. Their ailing pitching staff, and the tired arms of Don Newcombe and Preacher Roe, seemed to have their fix.

Then came September 21.

With the Dodgers' league lead down to four and a half games, the red-hot Labine took the hill to face the fifth-place Phillies. But in the 1st inning the right-hander found trouble for the first time in his young starting career, loading the bases and running the count full to Philadelphia's Willie "Puddin' Head" Jones. After a brief visit from manager Charlie Dressen, in which Dressen ordered his hurler to throw from the windup, Labine refused, sticking with what was most comfortable to him, the stretch. The next pitch was blasted by Jones for a grand slam.

That pitch led the Dodgers to defeat. And that afternoon's Ebbets Field run-in with Dressen landed Labine on the far end of the bullpen bench. The Dodgers would lose four more games to close out the regular season's end, including three to the Braves—a team Labine had dominated three weeks earlier, but the rookie was left in the pen. Instead of giving the ball to the fresh arm of the 4-1 Labine, Dressen sent Newcombe and Roe to the mound three times each in the season's final week and pitched Carl Erskine twice (both losses), with the second coming on just two days' rest.

The Dodgers' collapse was so complete, in fact, that if not for a pair of wins to close out the regular season, including a fourteen-inning nail-biter on the season's final day, the Giants would have won the pennant outright. As it was, the Dodgers went into the tiebreaking three-game playoff with a depleted bullpen and the momentum of a galloping turtle.

Without the home-field advantage.

That was heedlessly handed to the Giants when the Dodgers won the coin toss, but chose to play the first game at home and the final two (if necessary) at the Polo Grounds. Dressen reasoned that with a Game 1 win at Ebbets Field, his Dodgers would only have to win one of two on the road—an assumption that left Dressen and the Dodgers entrenched behind the proverbial eight ball when the Giants opened the series by beating Branca on the back of a 2-run homer by Thomson. A fully failed Brooklyn gamble that should have at least provided a beginner's blueprint for Dressen on the series' upcoming dos and don'ts. Instead, it merely foreshadowed the drama that was to come.

In Game 2, and facing a must win on the road, Dressen let Labine out of the doghouse. And if there had been any lingering concerns that the rookie was wilting under the parching pressure of a pennant race, and therefore didn't belong in the rotation as the Dodgers were limping toward the finish, Labine put those to rest, and then some, by blanking the Giants 10–0.

This set up the winner-take-all Game 3 on October 3, 1951.

With two aces on the mound—23-game-winner Sal Maglie for the Giants, and the Dodgers' 20-game-winner Newcombe, who at this point was running on fumes and on his way to a career-high 272 innings pitched—the game played out as a pitchers' duel. Jackie Robinson singled home a run in the first, with the Giants finally tying things at 1–1 with a Thomson sacrifice fly in the seventh. But in the top of the next frame the Dodgers struck for three, taking a secure 4–1 lead into the deciding bottom of the ninth, and seemingly leaving the Giants' 1951 miracle cupboard finally bare.

Newcombe, however, had thrown a complete game on September 29 and another 5⅔ innings in relief during Brooklyn's fourteen-inning affair on the thirtieth. And now, starting on just two days' rest, he had pitched eight innings of pressure-packed baseball at the Polo Grounds. He was exhausted. But the future MVP and Cy Young Award winner was also a champion. At the urging of Robinson, Newcombe went out to pitch the ninth and try and finish what he'd started, and send the Dodgers to the World Series.

But he simply had no gas left in the tank.

After singles to Alvin Dark and Don Mueller, a pop out by Monte Irvin, and a run-scoring double to left by Whitey Lockman, Dressen finally pulled Newcombe. The Dodgers still had a 4–2 lead, but the Giants had runners at second and third with Bobby Thomson, representing the winning run, striding to the plate.

The facts that Dressen had to work with when making his decision about Newcombe's relief were these. Ralph Branca was a good pitcher, except against the Giants. In 1951 alone, prior to his career-defining face-off with Thomson, Branca had given up 10 home runs while losing five times to the Dodgers' chief rival. He'd also been touched for a homer by Thomson, who was 2-for-3 in the game, just two days earlier—Thomson's second long ball of the season against Branca.

Yet with the season on the line and the Dodger-killing Thomson at the plate, Dressen chose to give the ball to Branca. And the rest, as they say, is baseball history—best immortalized by the often-heard call of Giants broadcaster Russ Hodges:

> *There's a long drive . . . it's gonna be . . . I believe. . . the Giants win the pennant!! The Giants win the pennant!! The Giants win the pennant!! Bobby Thomson hits into the lower deck of the left-field stands! The Giants win the pennant and they're going crazy, they're going crazy!*

If only Charlie Dressen had started Clem Labine another game in the final week of September . . . who knows. Or if Dressen had chosen one of his other bullpen options to face Bobby Thomson, instead of Branca, the man most likely to serve up the season to the Giants with one pitch . . . who knows. Or, with first base open, if Dressen had decided to intentionally walk Thomson and instead take his chances with twenty-year-old rookie Willie Mays . . . who knows.

We do know that no conceivable change in history's course could have matched the inconceivable actuality. In the perspicacious words of legendary sportswriter Red Smith:

> *Now it is done. Now the story ends. And there is no way to tell it. The art of fiction is dead. Reality has strangled invention. Only the utterly impossible, the inexpressibly fantastic, can ever be plausible again.*

Goat Trading
October 25, 1986—World Series Game 6, Red Sox vs. Mets

On May 2, 1986, thanks to a decision passed down from on high by very-well-paid television executives, Americans began mourning the loss of their *Fall Guy*. Colt Seavers (sometimes known as Lee Majors), using his dual roles as Hollywood stuntman and all-around bad-ass bounty hunter, shut down a morality-eroding nightclub and sent its corrupt owner to jail for selling PCP to impressionable kids. After making our neighborhoods safer, and our Friday nights on ABC just a little brighter, Colt said goodbye to us forever.

No more cheesy car stunts, no more GMC 4 x 4, and, sadly, no more Heather Thomas.

The same night we lost Colt with the television series finale, the Boston Red Sox lost 4–1 to the Oakland A's, dropping them to third place in the American League East. In that game first baseman Bill Buckner went 0-for-4 while stranding three base runners.

But Buckner was far from Boston's fall guy. In fact, thanks to

102 RBIs and 59 extra base hits, Buckner was very much in the good graces of Bostonians all the way to October. He was a key cog in the wheel that took the Red Sox from third place in May to just an out away from beating the Mets in the World Series, ending sixty-eight years of postseason misery and bringing good baseball times back to Beantown.

But in what stands as one of the most famous half-innings in baseball history, the bottom of the 10th of Game 6, after Wally Backman and Keith Hernandez recorded the first two outs, those cogs began to break. Gary Carter lashed a single to left. Kevin Mitchell lined a single to center. And when Ray Knight followed that with a single to center of his own, New York had the tying run just 90 feet away.

Relief pitcher Calvin Schiraldi had been solid for the Sox all season, finishing the year with an ERA of 1.41. In his one earlier World Series appearance, he'd pitched a scoreless 9th inning to pick up the save in Game 1. But in Game 6, he had already pitched the 8th and 9th innings, and—perhaps along with a little fatigue—nerves were setting in for the twenty-four-year-old.

Bob Stanley was Boston manager John McNamara's veteran in the bullpen. And Stanley was having a great Series. He'd picked up the save in Game 2 and had thrown three scoreless innings in Games 3 and 4. Yet McNamara waited until Schiraldi had been touched for three straight hits before making the pitching change. That was mistake No. 1.

Stanley, twice an All-Star in his career and a former starting pitcher with as many as nine complete games in a single season, was given the most important task of his life: retire Mookie Wilson. But with the count 2-2, and the Sox just one strike away from champagne—as they had been with Knight—Stanley buried a wild pitch in the dirt, scoring Mitchell to tie the game, 5–5, and moving Knight, the winning run, into scoring position.

Very few people talk about that wild pitch. Or the three straight hits that preceded it. Or McNamara's decision to stick with Schiraldi for a third, disastrous, inning after he'd already blown the save in the eighth. But everyone knows what happened next.

After fouling off several more pitches from Stanley, keeping his at bat alive with a 3-2 count, Wilson hit a soft ground ball down the first-base line that appeared to send Game 6 into the 11th inning. Then, in the blink of an eye, it was through the legs of Buckner and into right field, scoring Knight all the way from second base. Game over. Red Sox choke. Mets win.

And after an 8–5 Mets victory in Game 7 two nights later (rain pushed it back a day), the World Series ticker-tape parade was being scheduled for New York's "Canyon of Heroes." The city of Boston's October parade plans would have to wait another eighteen years.

The condemnation was swift and thorough and pointed. Buckner was to blame for the loss. It was an easy ground ball, he was a Major League Baseball player, and, with everything on the line, an error on such a play was unforgivable. Why didn't he get down on the ball—at least keep it in front of him? Why, Buckner, why?

But here's the real question. Why was Buckner in the game in the first place?

In Games 1, 2, and 5—the three games won by Boston—Buckner was on the bench by the final inning. He was playing on badly injured legs, having torn away much of the muscle from his ankle. And because they so greatly limited his mobility, McNamara had used Dave Stapleton as a defensive replacement when the Sox had a late lead. So what was different in Game 6? Why was Buckner still in? Extra innings, up by a pair of runs, with a chance to close out the season . . . surely that's the time to slant every possible percentage to your favor.

There are two possibilities as to why McNamara didn't make the defensive switch that he had been making all series. Some people blame sentiment. McNamara liked Buckner. He was a team player nearing the end of his career. And the manager wanted to let Buckner win his first World Series on the field and not the bench. Possible, and plausible, but not how you manage your way to a World Series ring—which McNamara never did.

The second possibility is that McNamara simply forgot. Considering the way he watched Schiraldi get touched for three straight line-drive hits, losing the lead for the second time in three innings, McNamara seemed more like a spectator in the 10th inning than the actual skipper. Also not how you manage a team in the World Series. Or softball beer leagues, for that matter.

Somehow, McNamara escaped the hammering Boston media. Buckner was run out of town the following season, released by the Red Sox in July. But McNamara managed his way through an entire-season fifth-place finish in 1987. In 1988, with the Sox still stuck in fifth at the All-Star break, McNamara was finally replaced by third-base coach Joe Morgan (not to be confused with the Hall of Fame second baseman who knocked in the winning run in Game 3 of the 1975 World Series against Boston after Cincinnati was given a giant assist from umpire Larry Barnett). Buckner finished his playing career with 2,715 hits. That's more than Ted Williams, Jim Rice, or Carlton Fisk. Yet those three men are Red Sox heroes. Buckner is unabashedly the ultimate Red Sox goat.

It's time the weights of that designation get deeded back to the man who doomed the frail first baseman: manager John McNamara.

A Not-So-Little Mistake

October 16, 2003—AL Championship Series Game 7,
Red Sox vs. Yankees

Along with sticking with Calvin Schiraldi one batter too many and inexplicably letting Bill Buckner play olé defense in the most important inning of the 1986 season, Red Sox manager John McNamara also is criticized for pulling Roger Clemens after seven innings in that same fateful Game 6. With a runner at second and one out, McNamara decided to pinch-hit for Clemens with Mike Greenwell in the top of the eighth. Greenwell struck out. In a cruel twist of irony, the Sox did end up loading the bases that inning, only failing to add to their lead after Buckner flied out, stranding all three runners. Oh so close to being the hero. If only.

The cautionary tale of McNamara's handling of his pitching staff in 1986, as told by his critics, finishes with a clear message. With the season on the line, stick with your ace. Clemens was the American League's Cy Young winner and MVP, as well as the All-Star Game MVP, and easily had the stuff to go the distance (even before he got connected with personal trainer Brian McNamee). He'd only thrown 82 pitches in his start six days earlier. And in the start before that, Clemens had cruised to an easy win over the Angels in Game 7 of the ALCS.

The bottom line: it should have been Clemens, and not Schiraldi, who went to the mound in the 8th inning of Game 6.

Of course, in the real world of baseball, there are absolutely no hard-and-fast rules to live by and no bottom lines, as Red Sox manager Grady Little would find out in 2003.

Game 7 of the 2003 ALCS was the most important game of the season for the Red Sox—and perhaps the most important game for the franchise since 1986. This wasn't just any seventh game. It was a seventh game at Yankee Stadium. The same Yankees who had been fitted for more diamond rings than Elizabeth Taylor, Liza Minnelli, and all of Larry King's wives, combined.

Grady Little and the Red Sox went into Game 7 with their ace, Pedro Martinez, on the mound and ready to go. But this was not the same pitcher from the late 1990s who would routinely complete games and throw 230 innings in a season. The Pedro of 2003 had to be handled with kid gloves. Still nasty, but with a much smaller tank feeding the engine.

From a pitch count of 85 to 100 pitches, opposing batters hit .230 against Martinez in 2003. But from pitch 101 to 120 that batting average ballooned to .370. He was a great 7-inning pitcher to send to the mound that Game 7, but after 7 innings he essentially turned from Pedro Martinez into a struggling Pedro Astacio. Not exactly the guy you give the ball to with the season at stake.

The first 6⅔ innings went precisely according to Little's plan, and held true to form for Martinez. Other than a solo home run to Jason Giambi in the 5th, not a single Yankee runner made it past second base. In three of the six complete innings, New York had been retired by Martinez in order. But in the 7th, with two down and the pitch count rising, Giambi hit another home run to pull the Yankees to within two runs, 4–2. Then the next two batters, Enrique Wilson and Karim Garcia—the eight and nine hitters in the lineup—got aboard with base hits. And suddenly Martinez was struggling to get out of the 7th inning with the lead.

But with the tying runs on base, Alfonso Soriano went down on strikes, and the collective cheer you heard coming from New England was Red Sox nation celebrating the seven innings their beloved BoSox were able to squeeze out of Martinez. The bullpen, a hodgepodge of cast-off arms that had been up and down during the regular season, had been amazing in October, allowing just two runs in their previous twenty-five innings, and surely they could get six more outs.

Maybe. But we'll never know. Instead of asking Mike Timlin or Alan Embree to protect what had been pushed to a 3-run lead thanks to a David Ortiz home run in the top of the inning, Little sent Martinez back to the mound for the bottom of the eighth. Both Timlin and Embree were ready—they'd even stopped warming up in anticipation of one of them getting the call—but Little was managing with his heart. Pedro was his guy. He wanted Pedro to get through one more inning.

Nick Johnson made the first out. But then a double by Derek Jeter, a run-scoring single by Bernie Williams, and a double to right by Hideki Matsui put the tying runs in scoring position with just one out. Little went to the mound to make the change, to finally end Martinez's day. Instead, he made the fateful decision of listening to his pitcher. Martinez knew he could get Jorge Posada. He could still get out of it.

But he didn't. On pitch number 123, Posada blooped a double to center field that scored both Williams and Matsui and effectively paid for Grady Little's train ticket out of Boston.

Tim Wakefield wasn't to blame for giving up the 11th-inning home run to Aaron Boone that sent New York on to the World Series. Martinez wasn't to blame for the four straight hits he allowed in the stomach-churning 8th inning. The ogre in this tale was no one other than manager Grady Little.

His players loved him. For most of the 2003 season, so did the fans. Public sentiment had been strongly in favor of the team picking up Little's option for the 2004 season. But the taste of that bitter defeat, seen by many die-hard Sox fans as the worst in franchise history, had to be purged from the system. And that meant that without question, Little had to go.

Little might have been judged more favorably by a different set of fans. But these were 2003 Red Sox fans—not exactly a group flush with the postseason success that allows one to be more forgiving. Sox fans burdened with decades of failure were quick to sacrifice any- and everyone who displayed the slightest hint of "the Curse" affliction. Good guy and good manager that he was, losing Little in the name of exorcism was a price they were lining up and down Boylston Street to pay.

"The Curse," as we all know now, was finally broken the very next year. The Red Sox rallied to win four straight games to beat the Yankees, 4-3, in the ALCS. And then they went on to sweep the Cardinals in four straight to win their first World Series since 1918.

That rather big bone *should* have placated the legions of bitter Bostonians. It, however, did not. To this day, the quickest way to spoil the appetite of a Red Sox fan is to mention the name Grady Little.

History Ignored
July 21, 1970—Mets vs. Padres

Grady Little averaged 94 wins in two seasons with the Red Sox. But it was his failure to make the right moves to win Game 7 against the Yankees in 2003 that defined his time in Boston. It wasn't just that he lost—he probably could have survived that. It was the way he lost. The perception was that he didn't do everything in his power to put his team in the best position to win. And that perception flies in the face of everything we believe in as fans. No matter which version you're familiar with of the famous Vince Lombardi quote "Winning isn't everything; it's the only thing," the meaning is crystal clear.

In truth, that isn't always the case. This dictate of success has been willfully violated time and time again. Because every now and then a lucky few get to put winning aside for something far more important to teams, athletes, and the fans who support both: history.

In 1997 Gordie Howe signed a one-day contract with the IHL's Detroit Vipers, not because he could help the Vipers win that one game, but so he could take the ice professionally in an incredible sixth decade. In 2007, with their week 9 game already won, a rookie star running back to care for, and a multimillion-dollar former 1,000-yard rusher also clamoring for carries, the Minnesota Vikings continued to feed the ball to Adrian Peterson—not to win, but so he could break the single-game rushing record. And when a Major League Baseball pitcher is on the verge of throwing a no-hitter, even when his pitch count is high and his tank is bordering on empty, he gets to take the mound in the 9th inning to try and finish the job.

Except if that pitcher is playing for Preston Gomez.

For those who don't remember Preston Gomez—which is probably most of you—he was the first manager of the San Diego Padres. The Padres were an awful team when they were created via Major League Baseball expansion in 1969, losing 110 games their first season and averaging 103 losses their first three years of existence. Gomez was the manager for every one of those 309 losses, finally getting a pink slip 7 losses into his fourth season in San Diego.

Winning in San Diego, while of course the goal, was hardly the only criterion. All four of the teams that entered the majors in 1969 became easy road-trip stops for the rest of the big-league clubs. And with the exception of the Kansas City Royals, who by year 3 were an above-.500 team finishing in second place (albeit 16 games back of the AL West–winning Oakland A's), the Expos, Brewers, and Padres all remained at or near the bottom of the standings for several years to come.

Fans certainly didn't go the ballpark in San Diego expecting the home team to win. Padres supporters no doubt found measures of baseball-rooting pleasure in places other than where their team sat in the standings. Like with Chris Cannizzaro, the club's first-ever All-Star. Or future big-league skipper Cito Gaston, the Padres' first .300 hitter and an All-Star in 1970. Or with Clay "the Kid" Kirby, who, while pitching against the Mets on the night of July 21, 1970, stood just three outs away from throwing the first no-hitter in franchise history.

As is the tradition in baseball, no one mentioned the no-hitter possibility to Kirby when he made it back to the dugout after striking out Tommy Agee to end the top of the eighth. Baseball, with its rally cap, aversion to stepping on the foul lines, and the often unhygienic practice of not washing a lucky pair of socks—

or worse—is by far and away the most superstition laden of all the major sports. You do not want to be the player who starts a losing streak by failing to tap your bat on home plate. And you certainly don't want to be the guy who jinxes a no-hitter by talking about it to the pitcher while it's still in progress.

So as the Padres began batting in the bottom of the eighth, trailing the Mets 1–0, no one said a word to the twenty-two-year-old about his shot at baseball immortality.

And apparently no one said anything to Gomez about the no-hitter possibility either, or its long-term benefits to the franchise. After Ed Spiezio and Bob Barton went down in order to start the San Diego half of the eighth, Gomez made the managerial decision to do anything and everything to try and get the win. With two outs and no one on base, and with the Padres a full 30 games behind the first-place Reds, Gomez yanked Kirby for a pinch hitter, who struck out.

Padres reliever Jack Baldschun allowed a hit to Bud Harrelson to begin the ninth, ending the no-hit bid, and the Padres went on to lose the meaningless game, 3–0, dropping the team 21 games below .500.

So I ask you, which would have done more for the Padres in 1970: a comeback win over the Mets, started with a two-out rally in the 8th inning that pulled the Padres to within 20 games of .500? Or having your young fledgling franchise get an excitement-inducing, publicity-making no-hitter from one of its youngest pitchers?

There are no "yeah, buts" to defend any part of Gomez's decision. From every angle, he made one of the worst managerial moves in baseball history. It wasn't a move that rocked the sport or changed the course of the 1970 season. But for a young franchise that drew just 10,373 fans to Jack Murphy Stadium that July night, a no-hitter would have meant everything.

It was also a move, inexplicably, that Gomez wasn't afraid to repeat. Four years later, pitching against the Reds, the Astros'

Don Wilson was losing a no-hitter, 2–1, through eight innings. Gomez was the manager in Houston in 1974, and with his team 16 games out of first place with less than four weeks left in the season, he pulled Wilson for a pinch hitter. The no-hitter was again lost by the bullpen. And again Gomez's team ultimately lost the meaningless game.

Sitting in the Cincinnati dugout as a member of the Reds, and watching Gomez rob a second pitcher, and franchise, of its place in the historical baseball spotlight, was none other than Clay Kirby.

Mismanagement

September 10, 1978—Yankees vs. Red Sox

When Preston Gomez was finally fired in San Diego in 1972, he was replaced by promoted third-base coach Don Zimmer. It was Zimmer's first, if somewhat brief, stop as a major-league manager. It eventually led to him taking the reins in Boston, where Zim bore witness to yet another Red Sox season that ended in abject misery because of a seemingly harmless swing of the bat. History, and especially the historical record as written by Red Sox fans, blames Bucky "F——ing" Dent (as he is known in Massachusetts) for robbing the Red Sox of their rightful place in the 1978 postseason.

It was Dent, the light-hitting shortstop, who had all of 4 home runs in 1978 before the one-game playoff at Fenway Park on October 2, who crushed the dreams of Bostonians of all ages with his pop-fly 5th home run of the season. It was Dent, the most undeserving of October heroes (in the minds of Sox fans), who keyed the destructive 7th inning with a wall-scraping 3-run homer over Fenway Park's Green Monster. And it is the mention of Dent, more than three decades later, that still raises blood pressures from Lexington to Framingham to Quincy.

But really, the vitriol felt for the man who now runs a baseball school for kids in Florida—complete with a full-sized replica of Fenway Park—is misdirected. The anger and insults should be reserved for the true culprit, the man who forced Boston into that one-game do-or-die playoff with New York: Red Sox manager Don Zimmer.

Today's baseball fan knows Zimmer as the pudgy former Yankees bench coach who got into a fight with Boston pitcher Pedro Martinez in the same 2003 ALCS in which Martinez was famously left in too long in Game 7. Or as the same pudgy coach who tearfully apologized the following day to his friends, family, fans, the Yankees, the Red Sox, the umpires, New York City bus drivers, people with birthdays in February, and cat lovers. It was an embarrassing display for the then seventy-two-year-old, both days.

But long before Zim was brawling with ballplayers half his age and blubbering before baseball's beat writers, he was the Boston manager. And as a manager in 1978 he had been gifted with one of the best offensive teams in baseball history. His Sox boasted a lineup that included Jim Rice, Carlton Fisk, Fred Lynn, Dwight Evans, and Carl Yastrzemski. As late as August 13 the heavy-hitting Sox had given Zim a nine-game lead in the standings.

Their pitching staff, however, was less than stellar. And managing both a rotation and bullpen was Zimmer's Achilles' heel—as was managing the egos and personalities that came along with being a Major League Baseball player in the 1970s.

Unless they are fresh off an early American history course, ask anyone in Massachusetts during the baseball season to explain the "Boston Massacre" and you are just as likely to get a retelling of the four-game September sweep at the hands of the Yankees that completely turned the tide of the 1978 season as you are to get a reference to the 1770 shooting of five civilians by British troops in colonial Boston. After all, one of these incidents changed the course of history while underscoring the need for the bravest among us to stand up and fight evil tyranny, and the other led to the American Revolution.

But if not for Zimmer's stubborn arrogance in how he managed his team, the "massacre" (we're talking about the one in 1978) need not have happened.

First, why on Earth Zimmer kept sending Butch Hobson out to third base each game is anyone's guess. Hobson was a fine hitter, for sure, but he spent the majority of 1978 playing with floating bone chips in the elbow of his throwing arm, which led Hobson to commit an incredible 43 errors. He was so bad in the field that season that his fielding percentage of .899 was the worst in baseball since 1916. And this was in the age of the designated hitter, when you could hide your all-bat, no-glove ballplayers.

Yet Zimmer chose to put Hobson into the field for 133 games that season, including all four of the games with the Yankees from September 7 through 10. During the four-game sweep Hobson had three hits, no RBIs, and three errors. Make that no-bat, no-glove.

But Zimmer's failure to utilize his other third basemen in the field—all were much better gloves than Hobson—was far from his greatest sin that season. In Game 4 of the series, after the Yankees had already shrunk the Boston lead down to one game, and the Red Sox should have been playing for a desperation win to salvage a least one scrap of good from New York's trip to town, Zimmer sent recently promoted rookie pitcher Bobby Sprowl to the hill for their most important game of the season.

By all rights, it should have been Bill Lee pitching. Lee had won 12 of his 17 career decisions against the Yankees. He was a solid veteran starting pitcher and had a good left-handed arm to throw against a Yankee lineup that featured the left-handed bats of Reggie Jackson, Greg Nettles, Mickey Rivers, and Chris Chambliss. But in July Lee had fallen into disfavor with Zimmer and suddenly found himself out of the starting rotation. Lee, not because of injury, suspension, or any doing of his own, missed six starts down the stretch. Even though he hadn't started a game since August 19, and had 191 career innings pitched against New York, he was left off the schedule for the Yankees series and completely passed over for the critical fourth game.

Zimmer also had Luis Tiant available for that game. Tiant threw a shutout against the Orioles on September 6, and having pitched on three days' rest numerous times (this was 1978), he would have been ready to take the ball to stop the Boston bleeding.

But Sprowl, a rookie who had given up four runs in five innings in his previous start, the first and only start of his career, was given the ball. Zimmer said of the twenty-two-year-old lefthander, "He has ice water in his veins."

Perhaps Zim was referencing Sprowl's inability to get warmed up, because the young hurler failed to get past the 1st inning against the Yankees. In two-thirds of an inning Sprowl walked four and gave up a hit, and before many of the fans had even found their seats, the Yankees' four-game sweep was well on its way to completion.

Sprowl would make exactly one more career start before leaving the majors for good in 1981.

With the margin for error so slim in 1978, with any one single win or loss the difference between winning the American League East outright or being forced into a one-game playoff, the responsibility for the collapse in Boston is Don Zimmer's, and his alone.

Eventually he did take Butch Hobson out of the field, and the Red Sox won eight straight games. If only Zimmer had done it earlier. And if Bill Lee had pitched in those six starts he missed during his banishment, he was a safe bet to win at least one. If only.

And if only on the most important day of the season—September 10—Zimmer hadn't played some wild hunch and handed the ball to a struggling rookie pitcher, but instead gone with one of his tried-and-trues, maybe Bucky Dent never gets an at bat on October 2. Maybe the Yankees' season is over before that knife through the heart of Boston is ever delivered. And maybe "the Curse" gets broken that October against the Dodgers, instead of living on for another twenty-six years.

Maybe. But we'll never know because of Don "F——ing" Zimmer.

Rotation in Ruins
September 21–30, 1964—Phillies vs. Reds, Braves, and Cardinals

Don Zimmer is the man with the distinction of having managed the Red Sox to the most memorable collapse in franchise history. But despite Boston fans and their notoriously long and unforgiving memories (see Grady Little), Zimmer has never received the full brunt of their fury. His decision to don Yankee pinstripes later in his career is far and away the bigger trespass.

Perhaps the only fans in America less willing to forgive a season-killing error in judgment are the levelheaded bunch that reside in Philadelphia—a group of fanatics at times so intense that if they needed something to throw at you and the only thing handy was a box of newborn kittens, get ready for flying felines. And that's no exaggeration. Why do you think the city orders all pet stores closed when the Eagles and Phillies are playing? *Okay, slight exaggeration.*

But, surprisingly, the worst late-September collapse in baseball history, which happened in the City of Brotherly Love, did not result in Phillies manager Gene Mauch getting run out of town on a very sharp rail. He amazingly lasted another four seasons in Philadelphia, which makes you wonder what was happening in the 1960s to make everyone there so unnaturally mellow.

Gene Mauch, any way you measure it, was a great major-league manager. He actually only made it to the postseason twice in his twenty-seven years at the helm—both times with the Angels, in 1982 and '86—but he always left a team better than when he found it. In his four full seasons in Minnesota the Twins finished above .500 three times. The Angels had been to the postseason exactly once in their twenty-year existence prior to Mauch. But under Mauch they were AL Western Division champs twice in his four full seasons in Anaheim.

In Philadelphia, where Mauch never made the playoffs, he was still a successful manager. As a rookie skipper at the age of thirty-four, he lost 94 games and lost another 107 the following season. But his third year, 1962, he began a streak of six straight seasons of above-.500 finishes. This was with a franchise that had winning records in just five of the previous forty-four seasons. Even with expansion Montreal, back when an expansion team (especially one in French-speaking Quebec) was an automatic cellar dweller, the Expos won fewer than 70 games only once in his seven seasons.

But it wasn't all good times and pleasant press clippings for Mauch. In the Expos' first season, Mauch had to endure a 20-game losing streak. And that streak, in 1969, was actually three better than the 23 straight losses his Phillies suffered in 1961—just one loss short of the major-league record.

But both of those losing skeins by bad teams pale in comparison to the 10 straight his very good 1964 Phillies dropped in the waning days of September. That collapse, and the decisions that directly led Philadelphia to cough up a 6½-game lead on September 20, with just 12 games left to play, haunted Mauch the rest of his life.

Just how comfortable were the Phillies with their late-September lead? They had actually started printing World Series tickets. And why shouldn't they? Third baseman Dick Allen was cruising to the NL Rookie of the Year award, finishing the season in the top 10 in batting average, hits, walks, runs, doubles, triples, and home runs. They had a rotation anchored by future Hall of Famer Jim Bunning, who threw a perfect game earlier that season. And left-hander Chris Short had come into his own by recording the third-lowest ERA in the league (it was 2.20 by season's end).

The stunning collapse started with the Reds in town and a heartbreaking 1–0 loss on September 21. Then the next night, with Short on the hill, the Phillies got rocked, 9–2, with Short giving up 6 earned runs in less than five innings. And that was followed up with losses by lefty Dennis Bennett, completing the Cincinnati sweep, and Bunning to open up the series with Milwaukee.

And then panic set in.

With their lead down to just three games following the four straight losses, Mauch went off script by sending Short back to the mound on just two days' rest. The Phillies lost, 7–5.

After another loss the next night, running the streak to six, Mauch went back to Bunning, also on just two days' rest. The exhausted right-hander, who would throw 284 innings before the season was through, lasted just three frames, getting tagged by the Braves for 10 hits and 7 runs in the 14–8 Milwaukee victory. But worse, following the game the Phillies found themselves looking up at Cincinnati in the standings. Philadelphia had fallen out of first place.

The team went on to St. Louis for three games, and Mauch, now desperate to salvage the sinking season, again chose to pitch Short on two days' rest. With nothing in the tank still, Short was no match for Bob Gibson and the Cardinals. St. Louis won, 5–1, pushing the Phillies streak to eight.

The following night Bennett couldn't get out of the 2nd inning, making it nine straight losses. And then it was back to Bunning for his third start in six days, and his third loss in six days. He gave up 6 runs and 8 hits in less than 4 innings, and the Phillies' season was over. The Cardinals, who were in third place when the Phillies lost their first of the terrible ten, would go on to take the pennant and win the World Series in seven games over the Yankees.

During Philadelphia's slide into infamy both Bunning and Short started three games. Bennett was a starter in two of the losses, despite an arm that had been giving him trouble since the All-Star break, and Art Mahaffey got the nod in the other two.

But what happened to Ray Culp? He'd started 19 games for the Phillies in 1964 and had beaten Milwaukee twice earlier in the season. At home, where seven of the ten losses came, he had a 2.50 ERA. While Rick Wise was just a rookie, and he'd only logged eight starts for the Phils, surely after witnessing the first disasters with Short and Bunning on two days' rest he'd have been a better option than going with them on short rest again.

And why wait five days to go back to Mahaffey, the tough-luck loser to begin the streak who had only given up the one run on a bizarre steal attempt of home that turned into a wild pitch?

Mauch was a brilliant by-the-numbers baseball tactician and the winningest manager to never win a pennant. But his nearly thirty years as a major-league manager will always, unfortunately, be defined not by 1,902 (his number of career wins) but by the numbers 6½ (games) in 12 (days).

Miracle at the Meadowlands
November 19, 1978—Eagles vs. Giants

The word "miracle"—derived from the Latin word *miraculum*, meaning "something to wonder at"—gets a wee bit overused now and then.

In the Culture Club song aptly titled "It's a Miracle," Boy George uses the word "miracle" a total of twenty-two times. If ever there was a case of hyperbolic lyric overkill, this is it. Unless,

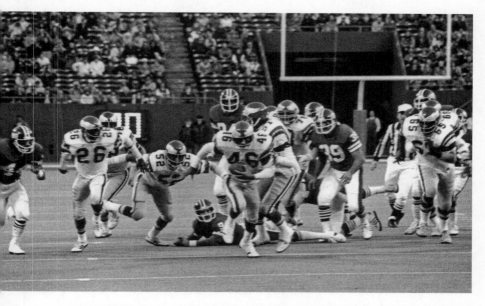

The Eagles' Herman Edwards (46) scoops up the fumbled handoff between Joe Pisarcik and Larry Csonka—a handoff that never should have been made—and sprints 26 yards to win the game for Philadelphia. *(Edwin Mahan/NFL/Getty Images)*

of course, he was singing about the likelihood of a cross-dressing androgynous Irishman hitting the top of the music charts with a song titled "Karma Chameleon," then twenty-two times may be a little light.

And George Foreman (with the sports celebrity's obligatory third-person reference) often calls himself "a miracle." I might be the first in line to declare that the Foreman Grill is a miracle of modernity responsible for providing sustenance to single men everywhere, while simultaneously taking them out of the drive-thru and into their kitchens. I, however, do not espouse the assertion that being large, aging, gifted with giant fists, and married to five different woman who willingly signed off on naming seven (five boys, two girls) of ten children George is a miracle.

But in the case of the events in the closing moments of a regular-season meeting between the Eagles and Giants that turned an otherwise mundane football game in 1978 into one of the most famous endings in pro football history, "miracle" is more than apropos. "Coaching buffoonery" would also fit, if only it alliterated better with Meadowlands.

The Eagles and Giants went into their November meeting as two teams headed in opposite directions, but both still clinging to hopes of a wildcard. New York was a team in turmoil, the loser of three straight, dropping its record to 5-6. Many of the players on offense had been openly critical of the play calling by offensive coordinator Bob Gibson, pointing to his lack of imagination on 3rd down during the previous week's loss to Washington, and his lack of confidence in Joe Pisarcik—a second-year undrafted quarterback out of New Mexico State who had to cut his pro football teeth for three seasons in the CFL.

Meanwhile, in Philadelphia, the Eagles and head coach Dick Vermeil were thinking about a playoff berth for the first time since 1960. Following wins over the Packers and Jets, the Eagles had pushed past .500, at 6-5, and were entering the toughest part of their schedule—three straight road games—with momentum clearly on their side.

The game, however, failed to reflect the rivals' current status. On the arm of two Pisarcik first-half touchdown passes, the Giants jumped out to the early lead, maintaining control throughout. Because of two failed extra-point opportunities by Philadelphia, the Eagles trailed late, 17–12, and were forced to try for a touchdown in the game's final moments instead of having a field-goal option that would then force sudden-death overtime.

Philly nearly got the break it so desperately needed late in the game when New York running back Doug Kotar coughed up the football deep in Giants territory. But that Eagles opportunity, and seemingly the game, slipped away when rookie defensive back Odis McKinney picked off quarterback Ron Jaworski for his first career NFL interception.

With Philadelphia out of timeouts and the game having moved past the two-minute warning, all the Giants' offense had to do was take a knee, which is exactly what they did on 2nd down. But in a desperate attempt to force a fumble, Eagles middle linebacker Bill Bergey—breaking unwritten protocol for just such a situation—plowed into Giants center Jim Clack, knocking him back into Pisarcik. Not wanting his quarterback to get injured, even though only one more snap was needed to kill the clock and the chance of injury was really quite remote, offensive coordinator Gibson sent in the play "65 power-up"—which called for a handoff to fullback Larry Csonka.

The Giants, naturally, were startled by the call. And the former Dolphins great is said to have reacted to hearing it by barking at Pisarcik, "Don't give me the ball." But as a quarterback who was slowly moving into his offensive coordinator's doghouse, and had just a week earlier been threatened with waiver by head coach John McVay for changing a play call that came in from the sideline, Pisarcik refused to go against his coaches. So 65 power-up it was.

The huddle discussion—and dissension—however, had used up precious seconds. And as the Giants broke the huddle, the play clock was ticking down dangerously close to a delay-of-game penalty—which would stop the clock and essentially grant the Eagles a bonus timeout. So Clack, seeing the play clock strike one, snapped the ball to Pisarcik before the quarterback was completely set—causing him to bobble the snap briefly and throw off the rhythm of the play.

That proved to be a fatal blow to New York's upset bid.

With the Eagles' defense on an all-out eleven-man blitz, Pisarcik, with a precarious-at-best hold on the football, tried to hand it to Csonka. Instead, he put it on his fullback's right hip, and the ball popped loose. After only one bounce, it popped right into the hands of Philadelphia's blitzing defensive back Herman Edwards, who sprinted his way to an easy 26-yard touchdown—and a miracle win at the Meadowlands.

It was, and is, one of the most improbable endings to a football game ever. And one that was missed entirely by Vermeil. The Eagles' head coach, thinking ahead to the torrent of criticism he was about to face for dropping the game to the reeling Giants, had already turned away from the field. It wasn't until he noticed several of his players running onto the field to celebrate that it dawned on him that something special—even miraculous—had happened.

On the other sideline, the retribution was swift and merciless. Gibson was fired the very next morning. And even though the Giants' management said the called handoff wasn't the reason, they did admit that he probably would have lasted through the season's final four games if it hadn't occurred. He never worked in football again.

Head coach John McVay did last the remainder of the season. But with the Giants again coming up short of the playoffs, and with fans in an all-out revolt following the humiliating loss to Philadelphia—which included a game-ticket bonfire in the parking lot before the next home game and a flyover banner that read "15 Years of Lousy Football—We've Had Enough"—McVay was fired. He never roamed the sidelines again as a head coach, but he landed on his feet. The next year he took a front-office job with the San Francisco 49ers and helped rookie head coach Bill Walsh build one of football's most successful dynasties.

The Giants' swift trip to rock bottom, and the subsequent housecleaning by owner Wellington Mara, did come with a silver lining. At the suggestion of Commissioner Pete Rozelle, Mara hired George Young as their new GM. Young's first pick as the new architect of the Giants was a little-known quarterback out of Morehead State named Phil Simms—the future MVP of Super Bowl XXI.

The Eagles, on a three-game winning streak following the "Miracle," used the furthered momentum to make the post-season for the first time in eighteen years. Two seasons later Vermeil, Edwards, and Pisarcik—now Jaworski's backup in Philadelphia—made it to the Super Bowl. Twenty-five years after that Edwards replaced Vermeil as the head coach of the Kansas City Chiefs.

Punch Buddy
January 2, 1994—Jets vs. Oilers

There have been a lot of famous punches thrown in sports, celebrated and otherwise. At the top of the list will always be the "phantom punch" that knocked out Sonny Liston in his 1965 rematch with Muhammad Ali. Just as famous, for a much more recent generation of fight fans, was the actual punch that left Mike Tyson's mouthpiece dangling and his heavyweight championship belt in the possession of 42-to-1 long shot James "Buster" Douglas.

In a very different context, the 1977 punch thrown by the Lakers' Kermit Washington that shattered several bones in the face of Rockets player (later coach) Rudy Tomjanovich will be remembered forever. As will the rather weak and flailing right hand that Oilers defensive coordinator Buddy Ryan threw at his offensive counterpart Kevin Gilbride.

That incident, caught on tape along the Oilers' sideline and replayed hundreds of times on ESPN, is the lasting image that football fans have of Ryan. In terms of his career, it is the one highlight that we all remember. Bears fans may point to his innovative "46" defense that swept Chicago to Super Bowl XX. A rare few may even refer back to his contributions to the defensive game plan that helped the Jets upset the Colts in Super Bowl

III, or his years in Minnesota as the coordinator of the "Purple People Eaters" defense in 1976 and '77.

Everyone, however, remembers the punch. A punch which, if it hadn't been for the greatest thirty minutes of Frank Reich's Bills career, never would have happened.

Led by defensive coordinator Jim Eddy in 1991 and '92, the Oilers had one of the league's top defenses. With William Fuller, Sean Jones, and Ray Childress on the defensive line, and Cris Dishman in the secondary, Houston went after the quarterback and consistently forced game-changing turnovers. And it was largely because of that defense, and not Warren Moon and the run-and-shoot offense, that the Oilers made the playoffs in both seasons.

As a wildcard team in 1992, the postseason road took Houston to Buffalo's Rich Stadium. But that January, a playoff trip to upstate New York wasn't nearly as daunting as it was throughout the rest of the early '90s. A week earlier the Oilers hosted, and hammered, the Bills, 27–3. The main reason for that lopsided score was the injury Houston inflicted on Buffalo quarterback Jim Kelly, which still had him sidelined a week later, effectively keeping the Bills' no-huddle offense in neutral.

As bad as the Bills' offense was without Kelly in the first half that playoff Sunday, Warren Moon was that good. Four touchdown passes had Houston up, 28–3, at halftime. And when Bubba McDowell intercepted Reich and scampered 58 yards for the touchdown to open up the third quarter, loyal Bills fans started fleeing for the exits. The Oilers were on their way to an epic demolition of Buffalo and to what was essentially a free pass to the playoff's second round. And all of the run-and-shoot naysayers were warming up a Hungry Man's portion of crow. The often-scorned pinball offense built for a dome was running away with a January playoff in the cold of Buffalo.

Until Frank Reich engineered the most incredible comeback in playoff history.

Reich had thrown a grand total of 47 passes in the regular season, none for touchdowns. In the second half against the Oilers, he threw four. In what can only be described as the biggest 180 in NFL history, Houston went from do-no-wrong to do-absolutely-nothing-right. They suddenly couldn't tackle or defend the pass, or complete one of their own. They stopped scoring, and the Bills couldn't be stopped. When the dust finally settled it was Buffalo moving on, 41–38, and Houston flying home as the laughingstock of football.

Someone had to pay. A head had to roll. A scapegoat had to be found. That was Jim Eddy. Never mind that his defense ranked third in the league that season. Eddy's defense had played its worst thirty minutes of football at the absolute worst possible time. To appease the seething city of Houston, Eddy got the sacrificial ax.

And in stepped Buddy Ryan.

Ryan came to Houston with an impressive defensive résumé and more than a little controversy. On Thanksgiving Day 1989, when most of America was celebrating the fall of the Berlin Wall in a turkey-induced coma, Ryan was allegedly paying his Eagles bonuses for taking out Cowboys rookie quarterback Troy Aikman and former Philly kicker Luis Zendejas.

For the purposes of maintaining some illusion of journalistic impartiality I'll stick with calling the since-called "Bounty Bowl" unproven. But if you ask Zendejas, a few former Eagles assistant coaches, and then-Cowboys head coach Jimmy Johnson, there was nothing "alleged" about Ryan's bounty. It was a fact. A fact that underscored Ryan's volatility and the "dignity-be-damned" attitude that he was bringing to the Oilers.

In the end, the change that the new defensive coordinator brought to Houston was negligible on the field. The defense was very good before Ryan got there, and it remained that way throughout 1993.

However, the Buddy effect, benign in the numbers, was downright malignant in the locker room. It wasn't merely Houston's next opponent that dominated Ryan's weekly focus. He spent much of his time and energy taking on his own team's run-and-shoot offense and its coordinator, Kevin Gilbride. Ryan often referred to the offense as the "chuck-and-duck," and he claimed that it was an offense for wimps and not real football players. Not like his defense.

Ryan also grumbled that Gilbride's offense wasn't any good at running out the clock. And it was this shortcoming, in the otherwise meaningless season finale for the already crowned division champion Oilers, that broke the camel's back and led to Ryan's most famous moment.

Late in the first half of Houston's final regular-season game against the Jets, quarterback Cody Carlson fumbled on a called passing play. Believing that all season long his defense was being forced to clean up Gilbride's messes, and blaming Gilbride for injuries to two of his players on last-minute defensive stands when Houston should have been able to run out the clock, Ryan began yelling at Gilbride.

Gilbride, who had had more than enough of Ryan throughout the season, refused to back down, and instead moved toward Ryan and started yelling back. After competing "I know you are, but what am I's," Ryan, in front of God, country, and the television cameras so conveniently provided for every NFL game, took a swing at Gilbride that was little more than a glancing third-grade schoolyard punch.

Players intervened and the two warring coaches were quickly separated. And the Oilers went on to close out the Jets and the regular season with what should have been a "Kumbaya"-inducing, 24–0, win. Unfortunately for Ryan, Gilbride, head coach Jack Pardee, and the rest of the Oilers, the media tends to ignore the juicy stories, like a win over an 8-8 team, and instead shamelessly focuses on the minor issue of two coaches trying to knock each other's heads off on the sideline.

The incident was replayed on television over and over. And after Ryan called Gilbride a "wimp" who should be "selling insurance," football analysts repeatedly called the Oilers a divided team ill prepared to focus on the postseason.

Owner Bud Adams, embarrassed by the controversy but unable to stop the bleeding in the media, issued a gag order for the entire organization, threatening fines to anyone who spoke on the topic. That did, effectively, end the quotes coming out of Houston. But it did nothing to unite the team for a playoff run. Following their first-round bye, the Oilers promptly lost at home to Joe Montana and the Kansas City Chiefs. Playoff failures in '91 and '92 were the only reasons that Ryan found himself with a Houston address. But because of Ryan and his divisive nature, the failure this time around was far more complete and lasting.

The team went into free fall the next season, turning their 12-4 record into a franchise worst 2-14 finish. Jack Pardee was fired ten games into the year (1-9) and had to take a pride-swallowing job in 1995 with the CFL's Birmingham Barracudas. It would be his last year in coaching.

Ryan had already skipped town, leaving Houston after the loss to Kansas City to become the head coach in Arizona. After only 12 wins in two seasons there, he was fired, sending him into retirement on his horse farm in Kentucky. There were never any reports that he tried to punch any horses, á la Mongo in *Blazing Saddles*.

The Oilers never had another winning record after Ryan's pestilential punch. By the time the team broke .500 again, in 1999, they were the Tennessee Titans.

A Fool and His Job Are Soon Parted
November 24, 2002—Lions vs. Bears

The American Heritage Dictionary defines the word "fool" as

> 1. *One who is deficient in judgment, sense, or understanding.*
> 2. *One who acts unwisely on a given occasion. . . .*

And sure, at one time or another, every single one of us could be defined as a fool. In certain situations we all lack judgment or understanding. But hopefully when it comes to our profession— something we are paid to be competent at—we possess both the understanding and judgment to stop from being branded a fool.

And most certainly when you are deemed to be one of the thirty-two most qualified professionals in your field, your judgment and understanding should never be in doubt. Each of us would feel completely at ease knowing that one of the thirty-two most qualified surgeons in the world was charged with our care. And imagine if you had access to one of the thirty-two most respected computer programmers on the planet each time you needed to call Microsoft customer support.

But the too-often-painful history of watching the football teams that we passionately and religiously root for long ago opened our eyes to the reality that the same unqualified competence that paints the rest of the world's elites does not extend to the thirty-two people who hold the most coveted positions in the world of professional football.

It was a cold and windy November day in the city of Chicago when one of those thirty-two mined even deeper into the depths of deficient judgment. Even to hardened fans, his complete and total lack of understanding of the basic principles of football was downright shocking.

You don't have to look much beyond Marty Mornhinweg's 5-27 record in Detroit to see his deficiencies as an NFL head coach. But on November 24, 2002, even his most vocal critics had to be stunned by the foolish and inconsistent decisions he made in the Lions' overtime loss to the Bears. They were the kind of mistakes that should be ironed out of existence when cutting your teeth as an assistant coach for a high school junior-varsity team.

Everyone's chief complaint about the NFL's overtime rule is

that in its current sudden-death format too much advantage is gained, or lost, by the simple flip of a coin. Almost a third of all overtimes never make it past the first possession—which, of course, always belongs to the team that wins the toss. It's why every off-season there is always a rumbling among the members of the rules committee that a new, more equitable overtime format is being discussed.

Wait . . . back up a minute. Did I say the first possession of overtime *always* belongs to the team that wins the coin toss? I meant always, except for this one really ridiculously dumb time when Marty Mornhinweg won the toss but elected to kick.

That's right, in the Lions' 20–17 overtime loss to the Bears, Detroit actually won the coin toss, but decided to take the wind and in turn give Chicago the football. True, it was a strong 17-mph wind. But by giving the ball to the Bears he was requiring that his defense, which had just given up fourth-quarter scoring drives of 91 and 43 yards that allowed Chicago to tie the game, to suddenly step up and make the stop.

And this was sudden death. First score wins. You don't get a chance at that first score until you get possession of the football.

Which, as it turned out, Detroit never did. Chicago took the overtime kickoff and marched down the field for a game-winning field goal. The Lions' offense never got its chance.

But that isn't the half of Mornhinweg's madness by a long shot. During the Bears' drive, with the ball at the Detroit 35, Chicago threw an incomplete pass on 3rd-and-8, and was also called for holding on the play. Since the incompletion set up a 4th-and-long, and the wind that was strong enough for Mornhinweg to value it over possession of the football was blowing in Chicago's face, making a 52-yard field-goal attempt next to impossible, it was an obvious time to decline the penalty and take the play.

Ah, but the mark of a brilliant strategist is to do exactly the opposite of what is expected. Instead of declining the penalty and setting up either a Chicago punt or a really long and risky 4th-down attempt for the Bears, Mornhinweg took the penalty to push them even farther out of field-goal range.

"I wanted them to have no or little opportunity to make a field goal, so I backed them up," explained Mornhinweg. "And again, I had confidence in our defense to go in and make a play."

Care to guess what happened?

On their 3rd-down redo the Bears picked up a big gain, setting up a very makeable 4th-and-short play, which was easily converted against the reeling Lions' defense. (Incidentally, the very fact that Chicago went for it on 4th-and-3 from the Detroit 30 underscores the fact that they would not have attempted a field goal from the 35.) Soon after that, with the ball down to the Lions' 23, Paul Edinger kicked the 40-yard game-winning field goal.

A still clueless Mornhinweg, while explaining his reasoning to reporters, said, "I would do that again. Well, knowing the outcome of this game, I wouldn't."

It seems he, like so many people, had never heard Mark Twain's famous (and sage) advice: "It is better to keep your mouth closed and let people think you are a fool than to open it and remove all doubt."

Shula's Slow Hook
January 12, 1969—Super Bowl III, Jets vs. Colts

I am a huge fan of cows. What's not to love about a single animal that can produce not only shoes, pants, and jackets, but nearly half the food pyramid? Your typical Ruth's Chris steak dinner involves a beautifully cut, seared-to-perfection piece of meat drizzled in sizzling butter that comes with either potatoes au gratin or a baked potato with butter; and you can chase the whole thing with crème brûlée or a piece of cheesecake. That's like a 90 to 95 percent cow-produced meal. I love the cow.

Sacred cows, on the other hand, are the kind of animals that should only be embraced after much skepticism and scrutiny. Sacred cows should be examined with a fine-toothed comb and always treated like a one-sided slant on history. Guided by that spirit of cynicism, please allow me to take to task some of the tenets that long elevated Joe Namath and Don Shula to a place of bovine reverence.

First, I should clarify that I definitely classify Don Shula as one of the best coaches to ever roam a sideline. He won an NFL-record 347 games, coached his teams to six Super Bowls, and twice captured the Vince Lombardi Trophy (Super Bowls VII and VIII). He also defines what it means to be a gentleman in the sport. He personifies class.

Shula also, however, was far from infallible in his coaching decisions. One such very important decision helped elevate the on-the-field legend of Joe Namath (slightly less the gentleman—see his drunken sideline come-on to ESPN's Suzy Kolber) to a level that perhaps wasn't completely deserved. I am, of course, talking about Super Bowl III and Namath's much-celebrated prediction that his underdog Jets would beat the 17½ point favorite Colts.

First of all, the prediction made by Namath, as described by him, was nothing more than a quick retort delivered at the Miami Touchdown Club three days before the game because a Colts fan said Baltimore would win easily. Namath has admitted that if not for that fan, he never would have made the guarantee that has since become the defining moment of his career.

Also, Namath was named the game's MVP, but he is the only quarterback to ever win a Super Bowl MVP award without throwing a single touchdown pass in the game. And Namath was by no means a top and efficient quarterback that year for the Jets. He completed less than 50 percent of his passes for the season and threw more interceptions (17) than touchdowns (15). With a career completion percentage of just over 50 (50.1), a career won-lost record of exactly .500 (63-63-4), and 47 more career interceptions than touchdowns, it's not a stretch, by any sense, to suggest that without the Jets' win in the Super Bowl Namath never sees the inside of the Hall of Fame in Canton, Ohio.

Really, the credit for that win should go to the New York defense and Don Shula's mismanagement of his quarterbacks.

Earl Morrall had been Shula's quarterback for most of the season because of an elbow injury that sent perhaps the greatest quarterback that ever lived, Johnny Unitas, to the sideline. And Morrall did have a very good season in place of Unitas, improbably winning the NFL's MVP award. But of the 10 straight wins that Morrall quarterbacked, the Colts' defense pitched shutouts in 4 of them, and all told just 7 touchdowns were allowed during the streak. Morrall was a good quarterback on a great team.

In the Super Bowl, however, Morrall was far from good. He was terrible. In the first half he misfired all over the field, throwing behind, and over, his players' heads. In the second quarter alone he threw three interceptions—including one on the Jets' 2-yard line, and the famous interception that came on a flea flicker that completely fooled the Jets, but saw Morrall fail to notice a wide-open Jimmy Orr near the end zone.

Yet when halftime rolled around the Colts only trailed 7–0. Their offense had been abysmal in the opening two quarters, but they were far from sunk. They had an entire half to make up for the one touchdown deficit and a healthy Johnny Unitas ready to come in and save the day.

But as the teams broke from the locker room and the second half began, Unitas was still on the sideline. Morrall was still under center, and the Baltimore offense was still scuffling. By the time Shula finally made the change, with the third-quarter clock at less than four minutes to play, Morrall had completed just 6 of

17 passes for 71 yards in seven scoreless Colt possessions. The New York lead had been pushed to 13.

In the fourth quarter Unitas was finally put in the game and led the Colts on a touchdown drive. But just 3:19 remained in the game and the Jets' lead stood at 16–7. It was too little, too late, and just not enough time for the future Hall of Famer to pull off the miracle and salvage the championship that had just three hours earlier been a foregone conclusion.

The Jets were Super Bowl champions. Joe Namath and his guarantee were the talk of pro football. The much maligned AFL had gained the respect of its older and previously better cousin, the NFL.

And Don Shula had gained a considerable amount of wisdom when it came to choosing a Super Bowl starting quarterback. Four years later, having moved on to the Dolphins, it was once again Morrall leading Shula's team to a double-digit win streak after an injury had sidelined the starting quarterback. But when Miami took on the Washington Redskins in Super Bowl VII, Shula returned to starter Bob Griese to secure the NFL's only undefeated season.

When Shula claimed Morrall off waivers in April of 1972, making him the backup to Griese, Shula said, "I happen to have a good memory. I remember what Earl did for me in 1968."

Both in how Morrall helped lead the Colts to the Super Bowl that season, and how he helped them lose it that fateful January day at the Orange Bowl in 1969.

Low Price

April 16, 2003—Arety's Angels Adult Club in Pensacola, Florida

While it can be painful to watch a person self-destruct and destroy his life's work, it is fascinating nonetheless. When a politician, nearing the highest levels of power and achievement, throws it all away for a handful of sexual conquests, we feel for the wife who is forced to stand by him in public support while her private life is laid bare for all to see. What is it that causes a man, so calculated and precise in his professional decisions, to have such capricious disregard for his personal integrity and his loved ones?

Is it simple arrogance? An exposed weakness? The intoxication of power and its possibilities? Or is it some other human frailty that is amplified by conceit?

Whatever the reason, it certainly isn't a disaffection that's limited to those in politics.

How many times have we seen the professional athlete worth $20 million forgo the $25 cab ride and instead choose to drive drunk? Or the good guy in baseball who seemingly had it all forever taint himself in the eyes of his fans because he cheated on his wife, Halle Berry? (I know David Justice has long since retired but I'm still at a loss. You were married to Halle Berry!) Or a coach, in his dream job or on the verge of getting it, flush it down the drain because of his own stupidity? Too many times to count.

When Blue Jays manager Tim Johnson traded in his major-league career for one in the Mexican League because the false stories he told his players about the battlefield horrors he faced in Vietnam completely ruined his credibility, we cringed. What kind of person claims to have shot a young Vietnamese girl when he never left California's Camp Pendleton?

We sort of sympathized with George O'Leary when the Notre Dame football job was taken away in less than a week, after his résumé was found to have been embellished. His fictitious "master's degree" from NYU had been added years earlier, when a high-profile program like Notre Dame never seemed like a real possibility. And his claim to have three collegiate football letters, when in fact he had never played in a single game, was fairly harmless. I'm sure if we looked at the résumés posted on Monster.com and totaled the number of Eagle Scouts, class presidents, and fluent French speakers, we'd find the tally impossibly high.

As someone who types 150 words a minute, is proficient in advanced 3-D web design, studied Hungarian tap at Juilliard, and spends six weeks every summer building homes for Habitat for Humanity, I invite those of you without sin to cast the first stone.

But in the case of Mike Price, it's different. The decisions he made came shortly after he'd landed the head coaching job with Alabama—a premier college football head coaching job if there ever was one. Price had just been given the keys to the castle after toiling for twenty-two years in Ogden, Utah, and Pullman, Washington. The then fifty-seven-year-old married father of three was living his dream, and the dream of almost everyone else in his profession. The head football coach at the University of Alabama is practically a state-certified deity.

Which must be why he wanted to be surrounded by angels.

It was at the Pensacola adult club Arety's Angels—the self-promoted hottest adult club in town, where it's "18 to party . . . 21 to party harder"—where Price met the many angels who would expose him for the mortal, and questionably moral, man that he was. While at the club Price is alleged to have spent a few hundred dollars on drinks and dance tips, and, in the words of dancer Lori (Destiny) Boudreaux, got "a little bad" in the semi-private dance area. And the story, told by *Sports Illustrated*, alleged that Price went back to his hotel room with three of the club's strippers. The next morning one of the women charged a $1,000 room service bill to Price's room.

The *SI* story went on to cite an anonymous source that claimed that Price and at least one of the women engaged in sex that night—a charge that Price vehemently denied. An article in the *Birmingham News* seemed to back up Price and contradict *SI* with its own source, Jennifer Eaton, an admitted Alabama football fan who claimed to be one of the women in the room, who confirmed that there was dancing and "carrying on" taking place, but no sex.

Eaton said, "He was very respectful. I think he was just a man wanting some company. I think pretty girls make him feel good. He made me feel good. Is that wrong?"

Yes, it is, when you consider that Price's attorney said in defense of his client that Price told him "he had so much to drink that he can't really say what happened."

Yes, it is, when you are the most visible employee of a state that treats your home like a shrine and your words like holy tenets.

Yes, it is, when you are married, the father to three children, and the man responsible for setting the moral compass of the eighteen- to twenty-two-year-olds playing in your football program.

And yes, it is, when you had already been warned by University of Alabama president Robert Witt about your prior behavior—which is alleged to have included drunkenness around campus and inappropriate propositions made to Alabama coeds.

Before ever coaching a game at Alabama, and before even signing the seven-year, $10 million contract that also said Price could be fired for any behavior "that brings [the] employee into public disrepute, contempt, scandal, or ridicule, or that reflects unfavorably upon the reputation of the high moral or ethical standards of the University," Price was removed as the Crimson Tide head coach.

Sports Illustrated continues to stand behind the details of its story. But on the revelation that *SI*'s source was never in the hotel room, and therefore had no actual firsthand knowledge of any sex between Price and the women in the room, Time Inc. reached an out-of-court settlement in the $20 million defamation lawsuit filed by Price.

Perhaps Price has his price, and the settlement money makes him feel a little vindication regarding the events that began in Pensacola and ended with his exit in Tuscaloosa. But to go from the Alabama head football coach, with the world at your feet, to a disgraced outcast forced to settle for the job at UTEP is evidence that the college football world will always place Price in the semiprivate room at Arety's Angels.

Woody Hayes Swings Away
December 29, 1978—Gator Bowl, Ohio State vs. Clemson

Through the years, flaring tempers have provided the sports world with some of its most entertaining and memorable moments. Tempers have, on more than one occasion, become an athlete's or coach's identifying brand.

The highlights of George Brett's Hall of Fame career are his .390 batting average in 1980, the batting titles he won in three different decades (1976, 1980, 1990), and his gold-medal-worthy sprint out of the Royals' dugout when Tim McClelland infamously overturned a home run against the Yankees in 1983 because of excessive pine tar.

Tony Stewart has an IRL IndyCar Series championship and four USAC championships, and is one of only fourteen drivers to win multiple NASCAR Sprint Cup Series championship trophies. But it's his multiple fines, penalty points, and probations from numerous run-ins with reporters, photographers, NASCAR officials, and other drivers that most fans think of when they hear his name.

Every bit as compelling as the artistic shot making and brilliant volleying that made John McEnroe one of the best players to ever take the tennis court was the abusive nature of his volatile temper, which led to heavy fines, suspensions, and a famous

Ohio State legend Woody Hayes is restrained on the Buckeyes' sideline shortly after punching Clemson's Charlie Bauman in the head. Restrainer Ken Fritz (56) was also the recipient of a Hayes haymaker during the explosive fourth-quarter fracas. *(© Bettmann/Corbis)*

disqualification at the 1990 Australian Open. Even Mac's American Express commercial has him contrite and hugging an old tennis referee (less-than-convincing actor portrayal notwithstanding) while making no mention of his seven Grand Slam singles titles.

But perhaps no figure in sport was ever so undone by a fit of rage, or had more of his great accomplishments overshadowed by a moment of insanity, than Ohio State football coach Woody Hayes. A firebrand of a man who despised losing and Michigan above all else, Hayes, to his ultimate detriment, was governed by emotions he could not control.

An English and history major in college, and with early designs on a career in law, Hayes began his college football head coaching career in 1946 at his alma mater, Denison University. A disciplinarian and perfectionist before the war, five years of serving in the wartime navy only reinforced those traits in Hayes. In his first year as head coach he was threatened with "consequences" by school administrators for being too hard on his players.

In 1949, after a pair of undefeated seasons at Denison, Hayes moved on to the "Cradle of Coaches," Miami University—adding his name to the likes of Paul Brown, Ara Parseghian, Weeb Ewbank, Sid Gillman, and Bo Schembechler as coaches who at one time called the school in Oxford, Ohio, home. During his short time at Miami Hayes also added to his list of temper flare-ups when, while in the athletic director's office, and in front of the city's mayor and a pair of influential boosters, the coach responded to a disagreement by smashing a trophy to pieces.

His next, and final, stop was Ohio State, described by Hayes as "the greatest coaching opportunity in the country." Hayes made the sidelines of Columbus Stadium his home for twenty-eight years. And for twenty-eight years he was as good a college football coach as there was. He won thirteen Big Ten titles, three national championships, and four Rose Bowls. He was also ever committed to his players' academics—even beyond their time at Ohio State.

A famous story about Hayes involves a former player who had moved on to Harvard Medical School but was thinking of dropping out. Hayes, in the middle of a heavy recruiting load, jumped on a plane to Boston unannounced and successfully convinced his ex-player to stick with it. That former player went on to become a top neurosurgeon.

Hayes was an enormous success on the field, his players graduated at a rate higher than that of the university's students as a whole, and in a time when racial inequality was the norm, Hayes is said to have treated both black and white players with equal respect.

But with the volatile Hayes there was always a "but."

In 1956 he attacked a television cameraman following a loss to Iowa. He took on a sportswriter three years later after losing to USC. And twice during the "Ten-Year War"—as the rivalry with

Michigan would be known when Bo Schembechler faced Hayes as the Wolverines' head coach (1969–78)—Hayes completely lost his cool. First, in 1971, he took future NFL referee Jerry Markbreit to task and tore apart the Michigan Stadium sideline down markers for what he thought were a series of missed pass interference calls. And in 1977, following a late-game fumble that sealed the Buckeyes' fate, he punched an ABC cameraman. Hayes refused to apologize for the assault, saying, "You get doggone tired of cameras being pushed in your face. I'm fed up with it. I make no apologies."

He was also kicked out of two Rose Bowls, including the 1973 game in which he shoved a camera into the eye of a news photographer. The Buckeyes lost that afternoon to USC, 42–17.

With Hayes there was always a "but"—be it his hot and mostly uncontrollable temper, obsession with perfection, or burning hatred of losing. And with three straight losses to Michigan in which his teams failed to score a touchdown and a subpar 1978 that sent Ohio State to the undesirable Gator Bowl, the perfect storm of Hayes combustion descended upon Jacksonville on December 29.

Trailing Clemson late in the game, 17–15, the Buckeyes and freshman quarterback Art Schlichter were given a final chance because of fumble recovery in Tigers territory. Ohio State faced a 3rd-and-5 at the 24. At the edge of field-goal range, the offense called a pass—the offensive play Hayes hated most. He often said of the forward pass, "Only three things can happen, and two of them are bad."

At the snap of the ball Schlichter drifted into the pocket, and then, fading back and to his right, the young quarterback tried to hit Ron Springs over the middle and in traffic. But reading the play well was sophomore middle linebacker Charlie Bauman, who stepped directly in front of Springs to make the easy interception.

The interception sealed the win for Clemson. But it was the

interception return, which took Bauman up to the 35-yard line, where he was pushed out of bounds and onto the Buckeye sideline, which secured his place in sports history. As the linebacker began to celebrate the pick and the win, the sixty-five-year-old Hayes impulsively ran up to Bauman and mystifyingly threw a punch to the side of his head.

The sideline immediately exploded into chaos.

Several Ohio State players ran over and tried to remove their coach from the scene—as Hayes held on to Bauman with his right hand. The refs got involved. A few members of the Clemson defense join the fracas. Finally, with most observers befuddled by the surreal nature of the events they were witnessing, sanity returned to the field and the competing sides were separated.

The final seconds of the game ticked away and the defeated and seemingly consumed Hayes, appearing visibly older than he had just moments before, shuffled from the field in a fog of confusion. No doubt he, too, couldn't piece together the line of thinking that in a split second took him from a respected molder of men to a disgraced senior outcast.

And all of it unfolded in front of a nationally televised audience, even though the man in charge of describing the images, Hall of Fame broadcaster Keith Jackson, never saw the play and never once made mention of it.

Alan Natali, years before he would write a biography on Hayes, described watching the televised self-destruction of the coach as "an almost hallucinatory experience. It was bizarre, it was unnerving. You knew it was just one of those epochal moments where, really, college football was not going to be the same after that."

When word of the punch made its way west to Pasadena, where Michigan was getting ready for the Rose Bowl, Bo Schembechler thought to himself, "It's over."

It was for Coach Hayes.

Before the Ohio State plane had even touched down from

its return flight home, the university had fired him. Instead of cheering fans and a glorious career-ending send-off for Wayne Woodrow Hayes, the heroic naval commander from World War II who had won 238 college football games and made the Buckeyes a perennial national power, there was only a quiet police escort waiting to take him home from the Columbus airport tarmac.

The following day Hayes quietly offered this self-analysis: "I got what was coming to me. Nobody hates losing more than I do. That's got me into trouble over the years, but it also made a man of mediocre ability into a pretty good coach."

Ever the coach, Hayes did call Bauman a few weeks after the incident. "He didn't apologize," said Bauman. "He asked what defense we were in."

Temple Temper
February 22, 2005—St. Joseph's vs. Temple

There are no excuses, ever, for a coach's lost temper flashing externally into the side of an opposing player's head. The smear that Woody Hayes's flying fist left on his legacy is well deserved. His career-ending act was an offensive breach of the coach-player entrustment. But it was a flashing temper, lost in an instant of insanity. While this doesn't make it excusable, it is more easily understandable.

But the allies, advocates, and apologists become much quieter when the act of aggression is premeditated. It's why our legal system treats planned intent very differently from impulse and reflex. And that's why, in the case of longtime Temple basketball coach John Chaney, the act that left a St. Joe's senior with a career-ending injury, and one of his own young charges with the lifetime label of "Chaney's Goon," is in its own class of shame.

During a Hall of Fame career that spanned four decades, Chaney won 741 games and appeared in seventeen NCAA tournaments. He was the nation's consensus coach of the year in 1988 and the first black coach ever to win 700 games. On the court he is credited with creating zone defenses that are taught by basketball coaches across the country. And off the court he is applauded for giving countless disadvantaged kids an opportunity at a college education that they otherwise would not have had.

But on February 22, 2005, he disgraced all of his good works by a completely classless and calculated act.

Chaney didn't hide his intention. The night before his Temple Owls were to face the St. Joseph's Hawks for their second meeting of the season, the coach complained to a group of reporters via conference call about what he deemed to be illegal screens by St. Joe's in the two teams' earlier meeting—a St. Joe's win. Chaney told the gathering of scribes that he planned to dispatch "one of my goons and have him run through one of those guys and chop him in the neck or something."

The line between fiery passion and afflictive violence can be thin. And it's a line that Chaney has crossed more than a few times.

In 1982, his first year at Temple, Chaney went after Stanford coach Tom Davis during a closely contested loss in the finals of the Stanford Invitational. Two years later Chaney went Latrell Sprewell on George Washington coach Gerry Gimelstob—long before Spree's much publicized attack on coach P. J. Carlesimo—by grabbing his GW colleague by the throat at halftime of a physically fought game. And who hasn't seen the 1994 video of an out-of-control Chaney raging in the postgame press conference at John Calipari, then the coach of UMass, and threatening to kill him?

Doing a spot-on Tony Soprano, Chaney screamed at Calipari, "I'll kill your [expletive] ass. You remember that. I'll kick your ass." As he was being dragged from the room by a number of security guards, who no doubt prevented Chaney from committing assault in front of two dozen members of the media, which in turn most likely kept him out of jail and in place as Temple's head basketball coach, Chaney continued to hurl insults and obscenities at Calipari, who he felt had intimidated the referees during their game that evening.

The punishment for threatening a fellow coach's life: a one-game suspension.

So, for some reason, despite his colorful history, which as most people know is the best predictor for future behavior, Chaney's very public notice that he was putting a "hit" out on a St. Joe's player was taken as nothing more than hot bravado from a cantankerous and aging coach. Even Chaney wouldn't cross that line, it was thought.

Oh, but he would. And he did.

The next evening, with his team trailing St. Joe's late, Chaney had seldom-used Nehemiah Ingram check himself into the game. In four minutes Ingram fouled himself out of the game, but not before getting his money's worth. Ingram's five fouls (an average of one every forty-eight seconds) included a swinging elbow to the chin of center Dwayne Jones and a midair hit on sixth-man John Bryant that left him sprawled on the floor for several minutes.

Two days later an MRI revealed that Bryant had suffered a displaced fracture of the right arm, ending his career early and leaving the Hawks short-handed for the duration of the postseason.

At the postgame press conference Chaney crowed about his actions like a proud prizefighter, and not like the leader of young men and responsible educator that he was paid to be. He explained, "I'm a mean, ornery SOB. I'm sending a message. I'm going to send in what we used to do years ago, send in the goon."

Chaney then added, "Ingram was not the only person I put in there. I put three or four players in there and was telling them to commit hard fouls."

Ingram is, however, the only one of Chaney's players to be tagged with the label "goon." And thankfully Bryant was the only one to leave the game physically injured. But what of the message that Chaney sent to the legions of Philadelphia's youth that look up to him? Or that the atmosphere that his leadership created had some Temple students spitting in the direction of Bryant and the St. Joe's cheerleaders and booing when Bryant was finally helped from the floor? Where is the accountability for that?

The following day Chaney decided to slap himself on the wrist by self-imposing a one-game suspension. That punishment was later extended by the university to five games (the remainder of the regular season and the duration of the Atlantic 10 conference tournament) after the extent of Bryant's injuries became known.

Chaney should, however, have been fired on the spot.

Chaney's supporters claimed that the good he did in his career was enough to grant him absolution. Never mind the fact that he directly led to the end of an athlete's career. Never mind that professional hockey players have done time behind bars for the same type of offenses. And never mind that he is not an NBA coach asking one highly paid player to commit a hard foul on another, but a member of a the Temple University faculty and first and foremost a teacher.

In the short term it was Chaney's supporters who won the day. Instead of the lesson learned being one of intolerance for this kind of planned, premeditated, and despicable behavior, Chaney was allowed to return to the school and coach for another season before finally retiring on his own terms.

In the long term Chaney's legacy will forever be tarnished.

He didn't actually throw a punch, as Woody Hayes did. But Hayes didn't end the college career of an opposing player by using one of his own players as a weapon of premeditated pettiness. That distinction will always belong to Chaney.

Party Crash and Burn
January 21–22, 2003—Iowa State vs. Missouri Postgame Revelry

It's a story as old as time itself.

An outwardly normal, middle-aged man suffers a heart-wrenching loss which forces upon him introspection about his lot in life and place in the world. This is turn drives him into a dignity-destroying midlife crisis in which he desperately, and quite pathetically, tries to recapture the spirit of his youth by reliving the days that have long passed him by.

Cinematically this timeless tale was best told in the beautifully crafted *Old School*. And Will Ferrell's powerful "Dust in the Wind" eulogization of Joseph "Blue" Palasky will forever rank him among the giants of his craft. Standing shoulder-to-shoulder with Colonel Nathan Jessep arrogantly avowing, "You can't handle the truth," cabdriver Travis Bickle's psychotic rant, "You talkin' to me?" and prizefighter Terry Malloy bemoaning, "I coulda been a contender," there is fraternity older brother Frank "the Tank" Ricard's emotional, "You're my boy, Blue."

There wasn't a dry eye in the house.

It was Oscar Wilde who first said that "life imitates art." And ironically, just one month before *Old School* had its nationwide theatrical release on February 21, 2003, the film played itself out in real life in the person of Iowa State head basketball coach Larry Eustachy. (Thankfully, minus the streaking, the animal tranquilizer dart to the jugular, and the 30-pound cinder block tied to your person in the most alarming of ways.)

Eustachy didn't K-Y wrestle any coeds. But as the forty-seven-year-old leader of a college basketball team, and thus a faculty member at Iowa State University, the things he did do were completely unacceptable.

On the night of January 21, Eustachy's Cyclones lost at Missouri, 64–59. The coach, as was his norm because he doesn't like to fly, stayed the night in Columbia while the rest of the team and staff flew back to Ames, Iowa. But instead of turning the evening into a late-night film session to assess the reasons behind his team's defeat, Eustachy traded in the solitude of his hotel room for the crowds and cocktails at a campus apartment party. Not a good idea when it's not your campus, your team just lost, you're a middle-aged man with a wife and kids back home, you're the state of Iowa's highest-paid public employee, and nearly all of the seventy-some-odd partygoers come equipped with a camera phone.

The photos and firsthand account provided to the *Des Moines Register* by Missouri student Sean Devereaux, a proud resident of the apartment in question, confirmed the initial reaction most people had upon hearing of Eustachy's revelry. Succinctly put by Devereaux, "[Eustachy] acted very un-coachlike."

Eustachy arrived at the party between 1:30 and 2:00 a.m. with Missouri player Josh Kroenke—Eustachy is a friend of Kroenke's father. Over the next three hours or so Eustachy drank beer, made disparaging remarks about his own team, and kissed several young women on the cheeks—by itself not the worst transgression in the world, but definitely embarrassing when color photos of the pecks appear on the front page of Iowa's largest newspaper.

The pictures from the night do look fairly innocuous. A couple of kisses on the cheeks and nothing more. But the account given by partygoer Elizabeth Noce, then a sophomore at Missouri, puts Eustachy's behavior that night in a much more uncomfortable light.

"We thought it was really funny that he was there," said Noce. "And then as the night progressed, he was drinking more and more. The comments he made to some of my friends turned inappropriate."

After getting into an argument with a student who wasn't so keen on Eustachy's presence at the party—or the coach being in the company of his girlfriend—and shunning suggestions from his own friends that they leave at 3:00 a.m., Eustachy is estimated to have finally left the apartment between 4:30 and 5:30 a.m. after he was escorted out to a waiting cab.

Shortly after that night a photo of Eustachy and a group of Missouri students appeared on an MU fan website. But it was quickly dismissed by the athletic department as nothing more than the coach taking a picture with fans who saw him out to dinner after the game. Then, a few weeks later, along with an entire series of pictures contrary to that explanation, came the detailed story in the *Register*, ending Eustachy's defense by university officials and creating a national firestorm.

But just as the coach was figuring out exactly how to deal with the party pictures coming out of Columbia, a student from Kansas State came forward with a story about a fraternity party in Manhattan, Kansas, that featured a well-known uninvited guest one year earlier. Nicole Wegner told the *Register* that Eustachy, again partying the night after an Iowa State loss on the road, made comments about her looks and how she was much too hot to be at K-State, and she should instead be attending the University of Kansas where the girls are much "hotter."

As a former University of Missouri student myself, and frequent visitor to the campuses of K-State and KU, I have to concede that Eustachy made a good point. But no matter how spot-on his evaluation of the "hotness" levels of the girls at the rival Kansas schools might have been, perhaps a frat party at K-State is not the place to make it. Although on the list of misjudgments made by Eustachy, his drunken critique of the comeliness of coeds in Manhattan probably fails to make the top 5. As does the fact that when he was being teased by K-State fans about the loss earlier that night, Eustachy is said to have responded, "My team sucks."

Eustachy, of course, did apologize. Or at least it was his version of an apology, given only after the pictures appeared in the paper, making all possible denials impossible. In a written statement Eustachy said, "I am certainly aware of the role drinking has played in my behavior. With the support of my family and friends, I will do everything in my power to make sure my actions reflect highly upon this university and this state."

Perhaps I've been jaded by the shirking of responsibility and the running to rehab that has become all the rage among the famous set. Actor Isaiah Washington makes an antihomosexual slur, so he goes to rehab. Former representative Mark Foley is discovered to have sent sexually explicit e-mails to a sixteen-year-old congressional page, and days later he's in rehab for alcoholism. Michael "Kramer" Richards goes on a racist rant that would make David Duke uncomfortable, and he goes to rehab for anger.

Going from villain to victim has become the most expedient way to repair your reputation. I will admit that this trend leaves me more than a little skeptical when it comes to Eustachy. I also admit that maybe that's not fair to him. But would it have killed him to say that above and beyond any problem with alcohol, he screwed up? Even if he was an above reproach teetotaler who had never allowed a drop of alcohol past his lips, he had no business party-hopping around the Big 12.

The carousing and consorting aside, Eustachy's presence was the mistake.

He did pay the price for his actions. He was forced to resign, something he vowed at the beginning of the controversy that he would not do, and accepted a cash settlement from the university. His contract paying him $1.1 million a season was set to run through 2011. Instead, he took $110,000 for what was left of 2003 and a onetime buyout of $850,000 for the rest.

Associate head coach Steve Barnes also became a casualty when he was suspended by Iowa State for reportedly trying to rally support for Eustachy and intimidate those who were against him. Barnes's moblike phone call to arms "to get those who got us" didn't sit too well with the man who dropped the ax on

Eustachy, athletic director Bruce Van De Velde. Barnes, for his part, said he didn't remember making the statement.

A year later, and after he had completed a monthlong inpatient alcohol rehabilitation program in Minnesota, Eustachy was hired as the head coach at Southern Mississippi. A clause in his contract said that any misuse of alcohol or drugs could end in termination. I'm sure that it was also made abundantly clear that drinking at campus parties and hitting on college girls qualified as "misuse."

A "Miracle" Helping Hand
February 22, 1980—Lake Placid Winter Olympics, USA vs. USSR

Fans of the Olympic Games have been privy to some of the greatest moments in sports history. Say what you will about Kerri Strug's voice; her clutch gold-medal-winning vault at the 1996 Atlanta Games made her a giant among Olympic champions.

In 2000 American Greco-Roman wrestler Rulon Gardner was competing in just his third international competition and had absolutely no chance against the Russian Bear, Aleksandr Karelin—the three-time Olympic champion who hadn't lost a match in thirteen years. But it was Karelin, who hadn't given up a single point in six years, who had to settle for silver. Gardner, in one of the biggest upsets imaginable, took the gold.

And even though it didn't air on American television until 11:45 p.m. on a Sunday night, the U.S. comeback in the 4 x 100 freestyle relay engineered by anchor Jason Lezak, and his fastest relay split in history, was the emotional highlight of the 2008 Beijing Games and the talk of an entire nation. The contrast of the uninhibited joy the four Americans—led by the most decorated Olympian in history, Michael Phelps—displayed in victory, as compared to the stunned silence that enveloped the four losing Frenchmen, who had so brazenly declared before the race that they would "smash" the Americans, captured the pendulum of emotions that makes sports so meaningful.

But in all the greatness that these triumphs added to the historical tapestry of sports, there is one swatch that will forever stand above all others: the "Miracle on Ice" at the 1980 Lake Placid Winter Olympics.

If you are a hockey fan, even just a casual one, you can no doubt name three of the men who in 1980 treated our nation to one of its proudest moments ever. Even people who have never watched or thought about hockey in the nearly three decades that have passed since America won hockey gold can rattle off the names Herb Brooks, Jim Craig, and Mike Eruzione.

But if you appreciate those three men for what they gave to the history of sports in the United States, then you must also recognize the contributions of Viktor Tikhonov and Vladislav Tretiak.

Tretiak is one of the best goalies who ever lived; and in 1980, as the goalie for the Soviet Union's Olympic hockey team, he was unquestionably the best net minder in the world. Tikhonov was the coach of that 1980 Soviet team and one of the best coaches ever to lead a hockey team. In his international career he won six golds in World Championship play and was an Olympic champion coach three times (1984, 1988, and 1992). Tikhonov is also the man who decided to bench Tretiak against the United States, forcing him to watch as a lesser goalie gave up the game-winning goal to Eruzione.

What prompted the move was a last-second first-period rebound goal by Madison, Wisconsin, native Mark Johnson. The original shot, off the stick of Dave Christian, was an easy save for Tretiak. But with the clock nearly expired Tretiak and a pair of his defenseman teammates relaxed. Johnson did not, and with one tick left before intermission the Americans had tied the score, 2–2.

When the Soviets emerged from the locker room to begin the second period, Tretiak was no longer in goal. Tikhonov, no doubt feeling the pressure of being tied with a team that he had demolished, 10–3, just two weeks earlier in an exhibition, replaced his superstar with backup Vladimir Myshkin—a fine goalie himself, but not the best.

And because of Tikhonov's knee-jerk goalie switch, when Johnson scored again in the third period to tie the score 3–3, and a couple of minutes later Eruzione scored to the send the entire nation into a frenzy over the 4–3 U.S. lead, the best the Soviets had was not on the ice.

Then came Al Michaels, with one of the most famous calls in all of broadcasting history:

Eleven seconds, you've got ten seconds; the countdown is going on right now! Morrow up to Silk . . . five seconds left in the game. . . . Do you believe in miracles? Yes! Unbelievable!

An incredible moment that still brings chills.

Tretiak, one of the few men to never play in North America and still be honored with induction into the Hockey Hall of Fame in Toronto, wrote of Tikhonov's decision in his autobiography, "I don't think I should have been replaced in that game. I had made so many mistakes already, I was confident my play would only improve. [Myshkin] is an excellent goalie, but he wasn't prepared for the struggle, he wasn't 'tuned in' to the Americans."

Years later, after Russian players began making their way to the NHL, U.S. hockey hero Johnson asked teammate, and former Soviet foe, defenseman Slava Fetisov why Tikhonov lost faith in his star goalie so quickly. Fetisov replied, "Coach crazy."

And like the phoenix, out of the ashes of one of the worst coaching decisions in hockey history rose one of the greatest sports moments of the twentieth century.

Le Prix de Fierté (The Price of Pride)
December 2, 1995—Red Wings vs. Canadiens

The lesson learned from Viktor Tikhonov and the 1980 Olympics is that you should never sit your star goalie. His place is on the ice. Always.

Well, not exactly, as it turns out. Mario Tremblay and the Montreal Canadiens learned the hard way that when it comes to managing star players there are no rules written in stone.

When Tremblay was named the Canadiens' head coach in 1995, he and Patrick Roy already had a contentious history. The two had been roommates when they were teammates, and Roy didn't care too much for the way he was ridden by Tremblay about his struggles with the English language when the future hockey Hall of Famer was a rookie. And Tremblay, who worked as a broadcaster just before taking the head coaching job with Montreal, had been publically critical of Roy.

The relationship continued to deteriorate from there.

During Tremblay's first team meeting as the Habs' new head coach—a hiring that Roy said lowered the expectations in Montreal—the two men had an angry exchange because Roy was laughing with teammate Mike Keane, and Tremblay felt disrespected. The two also nearly came to blows—twice, with the first incident taking place very publicly in a coffee shop.

Tremblay, convinced that his star player and Conn Smythe Trophy winner in both 1986 and 1993 was getting too full of himself, decided that when given the opportunity he would force a little humility on Roy. In the end, he decided, the health of the team is far more important than the ego of one player, albeit one of the best who ever lived.

On December 2, 1995, Tremblay was given his gift. The Detroit Red Wings were in town, and they were on—peppering the net with shot after shot and scoring goal after goal against the frustrated Roy.

In baseball, we all know a manager takes out his star pitcher on a night that he just doesn't have good stuff. The same unwritten rule applies in hockey. You don't keep you star goalie in the game when the only thing to gain is further embarrassment. But that is exactly what Tremblay did. He saw a chance to publicly humiliate Roy, and he took it—to the tune of nine goals allowed.

When Roy was finally and mercifully removed from the game, the seething goalie stormed past the smug Tremblay and went right to the box where team president Ronald Corey sat. Roy's words to Corey summed up the depth of the damage done: "This is my last game in Montreal."

And it was. Four days later, citing irreconcilable differences between their new coach and their star player, Montreal traded Roy and team captain Mike Keane to Colorado for goaltender Jocelyn Thibault and forwards Martin Rucinsky and Andrei Kovalenko.

Tremblay tried to lay the blame for the blowup on a Roy over-reaction, defending his decision to teach his star goalie a lesson by saying, "Maybe I could have told him to come to the bench after seven goals. I didn't. I waited for a couple of more. Two more goals, I don't think add up to a career."

But two more Stanley Cups might. That's how many titles Roy won with the Avalanche, including the first one just six months after he was traded to appease the ego of Tremblay—an appease-ment that completely changed the fortunes of two franchises.

In the eight seasons that Roy spent in Colorado the Avs won their division every year, advanced as far as the conference finals in six of the eight years, and won the two Stanley Cups. Mean-while in Montreal, over those same eight years, the Canadiens finished higher than fourth place only once, never advanced past the conference semifinals, and not only did they not play for, or win, the Stanley Cup, but four times they even failed to qualify for the playoffs—something that happened just once in the de-cade plus that Roy was minding their net.

Changing Hands

September 26, 2007—FIFA Women's World Cup Semifinals,
United States vs. Brazil

Patrick Roy's spiteful move out of Montreal and on to Colorado created one of the best rivalries in all of professional sports: Avalanche vs. Red Wings. During Roy's eight years with Colorado, either the Avs or the Wings won the Stanley Cup five times. The irony of the genesis of this rivalry definitely deserves note. If it hadn't been for the Red Wings, and their nine goals against Roy in December 1995, perhaps Roy never would have gone to Colorado, the powerful team there never would have been born, and Detroit might have won even more Stanley Cup titles.

Call it six degrees of rivalry creation.

In women's soccer the top rivalry on the world stage has gradually become the United States vs. Brazil. For years the Americans stood alone atop the world in the sport that they pioneered. But the dominance of the United States that was on display so famously in the Rose Bowl at the 1999 FIFA Women's World Cup is a thing of the past. The simple fact is that the rest of the world, in particular the soccer-crazed nation of Brazil, has some pretty good soccer players, too.

The tightened gap was apparent early on during the 2007 World Cup in China. The Americans had to score an equalizing goal in the second half just to salvage a 2–2 tie with underdog North Korea in their opening match. But from that point on the U.S. team seemed to right the ship, rattling off three straight wins by the scores of 2–0, 1–0, and 3–0, advancing its way into the semifinals against Brazil.

The Brazilians for their part had just struggled to get past Australia in their quarterfinal match. Although with that game coming on the heels of a perfect run through group play, in which Brazil outscored its opponents 10–0, the Americans had plenty of preparation to do. A date in the finals was far from guaranteed.

There is, and always has been, a very real disease that can unexpectedly afflict the finest of coaches, a syndrome with such strength that rational and intelligent coaches will suddenly buck conventional wisdom to the degree that any and all wisdom is nothing more than a distant ideal. It is called "overthinking." Paralysis by analysis, if you will.

Every soccer fan, player, and most certainly every coach knows that you do not change goalies mid-tournament for reasons unrelated to injuries or red cards. And on the eve of the U.S. match with Brazil, neither situation applied to goalkeeper Hope Solo. The twenty-six-year-old was completely healthy. Furthermore, she was playing great soccer, riding a scoreless streak that stretched back some three hundred minutes to the opening match.

But for reasons only known to him, head coach Greg Ryan didn't trust Solo. So, citing Briana Scurry's career record of 12-0 against Brazil, he went against all logic and made the switch in goal. Scurry, a thirty-six-year-old veteran of three World Cups and two Olympic tournaments (including the 2004 gold-medal-winning 2–1 game against Brazil), would start for the United States.

"I think the way the Brazilians play, in terms of creating off the dribble in the penalty box . . . I think [Scurry] is the best goalkeeper in the world in those situations," defended Ryan. "And if you could watch her in training every day and see the kind of saves she makes . . . I think it would be very clear to you."

But if it was really that clear, why wasn't Scurry starting from day one?

What was crystal clear, however, was that the Brazilian team was dictating how the U.S. coach was approaching their semifinal game. And that is not how a favored team should be acting, or reacting, on the eve of the biggest match of the season.

The next day the United States looked like anything but a

favored team. The Brazilians destroyed the Americans, 4–0, in a game that wasn't even that close.

"It was the wrong decision, and I think anybody who knows anything about the game knows that. There is no doubt in my mind that I would have made those saves," said an angry Solo after the loss. "You have to live in the present, and you can't live by big names. You can't live in the past." She was absolutely right. In 2007 Scurry was not the same player who shined in the shootout in the 1999 World Cup. And the Brazilian team that she was facing in 2007 wasn't close to the same team that she'd amassed such an impressive career record against.

You take Joe Montana over Drew Bledsoe, of course. But in 1994, when Montana was in the final year of his career and Bledsoe was making the Pro Bowl, in terms of a one-game starter you simply can't make that decision based on past accomplishments and name recognition.

That is what Ryan did. That is unforgivable. And that is why it was announced less than a month after the U.S. team's disappointing third-place finish that Ryan's contract would not be renewed.

Solo did apologize for her postgame comments, saying, "Although I stand strong in everything I said, the true disheartening moment for me was realizing it could look as though I was taking a direct shot at my own teammate. For that I am sorry. I hope everybody will come to know I have a deep respect for this team and for Bri."

The apology did not mention Ryan, and that apparently didn't sit too well with him. He compounded his error in judgment by dismissing Solo from the team prior to the U.S. team's third-place win over Norway, putting the future of the expected American goalie at the 2008 Olympics in jeopardy.

Luckily Solo didn't let Ryan, or his embarrassing dismissal of her from the 2007 World Cup, destroy her desire to continue on with Team USA. She stuck with the U.S. national team under new coach Pia Sundhage, going to the Beijing Olympics as the starting goalkeeper for the Americans. When the United States faced Brazil in the gold-medal game, it was Solo who held the high-scoring Brazilians without a goal for an incredible 120 minutes. With a spectacular save on a breakaway by Brazilian star Cristiane, and a stop of a point-blank shot by FIFA World Player of the Year Marta, it was Solo who keyed the American's 1–0 overtime Olympic championship.

As it turned out, Hope Solo wasn't such a liability playing against Brazil in a big game. I wonder if Greg Ryan was watching.

Human Pond Scum
Little League Baseball

It takes a special kind of person to be a good and effective Little League coach. You need to have an overflowing surplus of patience (like building Rome, teaching seven-year-olds to hit a baseball takes more than a day), the desire and ability to unconditionally commit your time and energy, and a clearly functioning moral compass for the complementary jobs of coach and adult role model.

Luckily, the majority of the dedicated men and women who coach youth sports possess these qualities. It certainly was the case with the baseball, football, and soccer teams that I played on as a kid. Anyone who has ever participated in team sports while they were growing up can clearly recognize the effect that these coaches had on helping to shape the kind of men and women that we eventually became. It is a tough and important role in our communities, and most of the time they fill it perfectly.

Rolando Paulino and Mark R. Downs Jr. are not two such coaches.

Little League coach Rolando Paulino and pitching phenom Danny Almonte received their keys to New York City, even though Little League officials were already investigating Almonte's age and eligibility. *(© Reuters/Corbis)*

In case you don't remember the name Rolando Paulino, and why it is that he gets tagged as one of the worst Little League baseball coaches ever, perhaps you remember his most famous player, Danny Almonte—the Dominican sensation who moved to the Bronx in 2000 and by 2001 was leading the Rolando Paulino All-Stars to baseball stardom.

When combined with the shorter distance from the pitching mound to home plate, Almonte's 75-mph fastball was the equivalent of a 97-mph major-league fastball. Naturally, the 5-foot-8 lefthander absolutely dominated the other twelve-year-olds he faced—leading the Bronx team to district, sectional, and regional tournament wins and a third-place finish at the Little League World Series.

In three starts in Williamsport, Pennsylvania, Almonte struck out an eye-popping 62 of the 72 batters he faced and allowed just three hits in three starts—all without yielding a single earned run. The "Little Unit," as he was called because of the comparisons to Randy Johnson, was a national sensation. His team had so captured the hearts of New Yorkers that before a Yankees game shortly after the Little League World Series was over, Mayor Rudy Giuliani gave them the key to the city.

But, of course, that was barely half of the story. From that high in Yankee Stadium, the fall was far. Prompted by suspicions that not everything with Paulino's team was on the up-and-up, investigators went to the Dominican Republic and discovered that Almonte was not twelve, but fourteen. His birth certificate had been faked. Even as Almonte's father, Felipe, went on *Good Morning America* to proclaim his son's innocence, the deception had unraveled.

Finally, and officially, Little League baseball declared Almonte ineligible retroactively, meaning that every win and every record that the team from the Bronx had set was wiped clean from the books.

The blame doesn't lay with Almonte, a kid trying to please his father and coach. Even Felipe Almonte, no doubt a big villain in this, gets some reprieve because he could justify his actions to himself as an attempt to help his son. It doesn't give him absolution by any stretch, but an ever so tiny measure of understanding. But Paulino was supposed to have the good of the team and *all* of his players as his number one concern. Because he allowed this ruse to play out, the celebrated accomplishments the other members of his team had the right to be proud of were made meaningless.

And that's to say nothing of the teams that lost to Paulino's All-Stars along the way and were robbed of their rightful opportunities to themselves make it to the Little League World Series. The number of boys who lost out on a dream's possible fulfillment because of Paulino is too high to count.

Paulino sold his own integrity for the opportunity to win a Little League World Series title, and that is bad enough. But worse, his actions also brought into question the integrity of a bunch of innocent twelve-year-olds. He claims to be a victim as well, but that's not how it looks from where I'm sitting.

It is that victimization of otherwise innocent children that also warrants a spot for Mark R. Downs Jr. among these pages of illumination. If you believe there is a hell, then you must also believe that there is a special room in it for people like Downs. As a Little League coach in Pennsylvania, Downs offered to pay one of his nine-year-old players $25 to intentionally injure another of his players.

Oh, but it gets worse.

You see, Downs's team was on the verge of making it to the championship game. But he was afraid that a league requirement that each player get into the game for at least three innings was going to hurt his chances to win. Because that meant Harry Bowers, an autistic eight-year-old, would have to play.

The first thrown ball fired by Downs's "hit man" during pre-game warm-ups nailed Bowers in the groin. It hurt him—he went to his mother crying. But it didn't knock him out of the game. Bowers's mother convinced the young boy that he should get back on the field because it could only have been an accident. But, as the player doing the throwing testified later in court, Downs told him "to go back out there and hit him harder."

The next thrown ball struck Bowers in the ear.

Thankfully the despicable Downs did not go unpunished. He was arrested, charged, tried, and convicted of corruption of minors and criminal solicitation to commit simple assault. And he was in turn sent to prison.

But leaving no doubt that he is in fact one of the worst human beings walking around today, and that rehabilitation is not in the cards for this lord of the douche bags, Downs not only refused to take a plea bargain that would have shortened his sentence and spared the two children from having to testify in court, he appealed his case all the way to the state Superior Court.

Nearly three full years after Downs so boldly summited the peak of Mount Depravity by putting his own need to fill his empty soul with a meaningless win above the health and well-being of two children, his final appeals were denied.

Upon the revocation of his bond that sent him to prison, Mark R. Downs Jr. said, "I didn't do nothing."

Is it wrong of me to hope that in prison he is blessed with a very large and amorous cell mate?

THE FRONT OFFICE

While the roots of fantasy baseball go all the way back to the early 1960s and a group of professors at Harvard University, the true innovation began in 1980, when writer Daniel Okrent and his friends created a league that didn't just compile season-ending stats, like the Harvard guys, but actually tabulated statistics during the season so the friends could keep track of their ongoing scores. The group would meet and play its new baseball game at a restaurant in New York called La Rotisserie Française.

And Rotisserie baseball was born.

By 1981 major sports publications were writing about Rotisserie baseball. In 1984 the founders of the phenomenon had published a complete book of rules and player rankings. And by 1988 *USA Today* estimated that there were nearly 500,000 players nationwide.

Fantasy football was also beginning to boom in the 1980s. The earliest-known league dates all the way back to 1962, but it lived in obscurity among a small group of Oakland Raiders employees and area sportswriters. But with computers came easier stat keeping. With the Internet, player information and leagues exploded nationwide. And the Fantasy Sports Trade Association (you're big when you have your own association) estimates that in 2007 there were 29.9 million people above the age of twelve in Canada and the United States who were active fantasy sports participants.

That adds up to a nearly $4 billion economic impact for the North American sports world.

It seems that in every sport, from baseball and football to golf and NASCAR and everything in between, fans from all walks of life want to run their own sports franchise. They want to draft. They want to trade. And they all want to be the team owner who finds that overlooked and underrated free agent gem.

And why shouldn't there be 29.9 million amateur GMs? They can't be any worse than the professionals.

No, No, Nanette
December 26, 1919—Yankees and Red Sox

As human beings we pride ourselves on our reason. The instincts drawn from the inherent trait of being reasonable are one of the things we use for survival. It's impossible to survive professionally if you don't deal with your boss reasonably, even in the face of his or her own unreasonable actions. When trying to work a negotiation—be it with a new-car salesman or a ticket scalper, or in the "please meet me halfway on this weekend's movie selection" back-and-forth that all men have with their wives—unreasonable demands are self-defeating, and more often than not result in you getting nothing—or worse, you getting two hours of Jennifer Lopez as an unlucky-in-love wedding planner. (Kill me now.)

Reason is also critical when star athletes and the owners who pay them sit down at the negotiating table. And just like trying to explain to your wife the dramatic qualities of the love that is shared between Rambo and his gun, team-player negotiations have to be handled delicately. Egos are involved, and the balance of power is forever shifting.

When Babe Ruth went to the Red Sox in 1919 and demanded a raise from $10,000 a season to $20,000, he had the power. In the Red Sox World Series wins in 1916 and 1918, Ruth was a star on the mound. In his three starts—three of the eight Boston wins (including a 14-inning complete game)—he had a combined ERA of 0.87. And that came on the heels of two 20-plus-win seasons with the Sox, a regular-season ERA title in 1916, two seasons of more than 300 innings pitched, and a 2.22 ERA in 1918—the same season he tied for the major-league lead with 11 home runs and finished in the top 5 in the American League in both doubles and triples.

Did I mention that in the 1919 season, when he still threw more than 133 innings and won 9 games as a starting pitcher, he hit a single-season record 29 home runs—more than the total hit by 10 of the 15 other teams in baseball, and 88 percent of the total home runs hit by Boston?

So when Ruth, the unquestioned best player in baseball who was still just twenty-four years old, demanded a raise from team owner Harry Frazee, he was being completely reasonable. But Frazee would hear none of it, refusing to meet Ruth's demand and immediately setting on a course to find a partner to trade with.

Along with the Red Sox, Frazee was heavily invested in the theater. He'd produced a number of Broadway hits earlier in the decade, but by 1919 he was hurting financially and in need of an influx of cash. So when comparing the two serious offers he'd received for Ruth—the White Sox offered up $60,000 and Shoeless Joe Jackson (he wouldn't be suspended from baseball until September 1920), while the Yankees put on the table a cash offer of $125,000 and a loan of $300,000, with the mortgage of

Fenway Park as collateral—Frazee jumped at the New York deal, which was finalized the night of December 26, 1919.

When it was announced ten days later, Frazee told the *Boston Globe*:

> *No other club could afford to give me the amount the Yankees have paid for [Ruth], and I don't mind saying I think they are taking a gamble. With this money the Boston club can now go into the market and buy other players and have a stronger and better team in all respects than we would have if Ruth had remained with us.*

I'll let the numbers be the judge of whether that is in fact what happened.

From their first season in 1901 to Ruth's final season in Boston in 1919, the Red Sox won six American League championships and five World Series crowns. During the fifteen years Ruth played with the Yankees the Red Sox never finished higher than fourth place, and they finished dead last in nine of those fifteen seasons. And, of course, they wouldn't win another World Series until 2004—eighty-five years after trading Babe Ruth.

Meanwhile the Yankees, who never made an appearance in the postseason during their nineteen years of existence before Babe Ruth, would win seven pennants and four World Series titles with Ruth in their everyday lineup. By the time the Red Sox finally broke "the Curse" in 2004 the Yankees had amassed twenty-six world championships.

And as for that team investing that Frazee told the city of Boston he planned to do with the cash he got for Ruth . . . it turns out the Broadway stage play *My Lady Friends*—which was a nonmusical precursor to the popular musical *No, No, Nanette* (the latter debuted on Broadway in 1925 and had film adaptations in 1930 and 1940)—was financed by the Babe Ruth trade.

I've never seen *No, No, Nanette*. So I can't speak to whether or not it is a "Ruthian" triumph of the stage. But my *Baseball Encyclopedia* tells me that in 1920 Ruth debuted with the Yankees by hitting 54 home runs. The entire Red Sox team hit 22 that year. In 1921 Ruth hit 59 home runs. The Red Sox had 17.

In fact, during the fifteen years that Ruth played for the Yankees, he hit a total of 659 home runs. Over those same fifteen years the Sox as a team hit 553.

There's no, no way that *No, No, Nanette* was that good.

A Long and Sunny "Twilight"
Dan Duquette and Roger Clemens

Sticks and stones may break my bones, but words will haunt me forever.

So goes the lesser-known version of the childhood taunt.

Just ask quarterback Matt Hasselbeck about the truth of this parlance. He could win every Super Bowl from here to football immortality, but he will always be the guy who announced to a national television audience upon winning a playoff overtime coin toss in Green Bay, "We want the ball, and we're going to win!"

Then four minutes into that overtime he threw an interception that was returned for a Packers touchdown and a Seahawks loss.

But no one seems to remember that it was Hasselbeck who orchestrated a final-minute drive in regulation to tie the game and force overtime. Or that two years later it was Hasselbeck who led the NFL's highest-scoring offense to the Super Bowl. Instead, he will always be that guy standing on the 50-yard line of Lambeau Field, defined by an excited utterance.

Likewise, when it comes to former Red Sox general manager Dan Duquette, no one talks about his acquisitions of Pedro Martinez, Manny Ramirez, and Jason Varitek—all major contributors to the team's World Series win in 2004, two years after Duquette was fired by new ownership. He also is the man who traded for Derek Lowe, who went on to become the first and only pitcher in history to win the closing games in three post-season series in a single season. Lowe closed out the Angels in the ALDS, the Yankees in the ALCS, and the Cardinals in Game 4 of the World Series.

Instead, when most fans hear the name Dan Duquette they immediately remember that it was he who made the decision to usher the then thirty-four-year-old Roger Clemens out of Boston in 1996, famously saying, "The Red Sox and our fans were fortunate to see Roger Clemens play in his prime, and we had hoped to keep him in Boston during the twilight of his career."

On the surface it's not the worst thing ever said about a player by a GM. But the use of the word "twilight" gave us immediate insight into how Duquette approached his contract negotiations with Clemens's agent. Duquette was trying to diminish the value of the future Roger Clemens.

Since we now know what the true value of the future Clemens was—four more Cy Young Awards, 162 more wins, and 2,082 more strikeouts—Duquette's words ring ridiculous. He made a terrible decision in letting Clemens walk to Toronto, forever tainting his tenure with the Sox. And to suggest that it was anything but a boneheaded move on his part is disingenuous.

Clemens must have been asking for too much money, you might be thinking.

Wrong. Duquette proudly proclaimed that he had offered Clemens the richest contract in team history—four years for $22 million (he signed with the Blue Jays for three years with $24.75 million guaranteed). But the Sox offer of $5.5 million a season was the same exact figure Clemens had made the previous two seasons. And when Pedro Martinez began his Red Sox career in 1998, he was paid $7.575 million. Clearly the team could have offered more.

Then Clemens's skills must have been declining. After all, he had a losing record in 1996.

Wrong. Yes, he did have a losing record (10-13) in 1996, but every good general manager knows—especially the ones who listen to the guru of statistical player evaluations, Bill James—that a simple tally of wins and losses is a terrible way to measure the worth of a player. Sportswriters haven't seemed to figure that out yet, weighing wins far too heavily when picking a Cy Young winner (think Jack McDowell), but a good GM understands that wins and losses rely on too many external factors beyond a pitcher's control.

In 1996 Clemens's 257 strikeouts and 9.53 strikeouts per nine innings both led the league, proving that he was still incredibly difficult to hit. He also ranked fifth in innings pitched (242.6) and sixth in ERA (3.63), evidence that he was a still a durable starting pitcher who was incredibly difficult to score against. Sure, his ERA was a little up from where it had been five years earlier, but so was everyone's. After all, 1996 was the year that Brady Anderson, who averaged just 12 home runs in his thirteen other full major-league seasons, hit an astounding 50 home runs. Offense was off the charts across the board. And while Clemens's ERA did go up, only five pitchers in the American League were better.

Sammy Ellis, the Red Sox pitching coach in 1996, said he "couldn't believe" the Red Sox would say good-bye to Clemens. Not only had Ellis reported to Duquette and company that Clemens was still throwing between 94 and 96 mph from a game's start to finish, but in his final win with Boston on September 18, 1996, he matched his own major-league record by striking out twenty Detroit Tigers.

Duquette apologists now point to the Mitchell Report and the stink of steroid use that presently swirls around Clemens. They say that Duquette was right, and only illegal drug use kept Clemens going for another decade. And would the Red Sox really want to be associated with that mess?

Even noted longtime broadcaster and baseball fan Bob Costas has bought into this fairy tale. Costas said of the Mitchell Report, "This information certainly makes Duquette look better. Roger was looking for an enormous contract while coming off a poor year. [Poor? Look at the numbers, Bob. I expect better from you.] He was a power pitcher, and it could be theorized he was on the decline."

It was also theorized at one time that the sun revolved around Earth, but we still don't defend the church for jailing Galileo. In the face of the incontrovertible evidence that Clemens was not in fact "on the decline," the defense of Duquette has to cease.

It should also be noted that Brian McNamee told Mitchell's investigators that he didn't inject Clemens with steroids until 1998, the season *after* he kicked off his "twilight" years in Toronto with 21 wins, a 2.05 ERA, and his fourth Cy Young Award.

There is no black eye on the Blue Jays for employing Clemens in '97 and '98. The issues between Clemens, McNamee, and former senator George Mitchell have nothing to do with them. That same atmosphere of amnesty would have extended to the Red Sox had they rightly kept the Rocket in Boston.

Absolution, however, should not be given to Duquette. He made a tragically flawed miscalculation based on nothing, and made it notably worse by the choice of words that will now haunt him forever.

Amazin' Miscues
1966 Amateur Draft; December 10, 1971; June 15, 1977—Mets

The fact that the Mets have been involved in some of the worst personnel decisions in baseball history isn't news to any of their fans. But to those of us who are not devotees of the New York Metropolitans, the short list of their front-office failures is downright jaw-dropping. There is no doubt that the depth and breadth of these head-scratchers is one of the big reasons that the Mets are constantly playing second fiddle to their crosstown older brothers, the Yankees.

Hall of Famers are hard enough to unearth. Homegrown Cooperstown-bound prospects are generational finds that should be held onto with the grip of a man dangling from a New York skyscraper. Yet in just over a decade the Mets traded away two such players and passed on drafting a third.

For some perspective, of the thirteen other franchises that have entered the major leagues since the 1960s, only the Royals, Brewers, Expos/Nationals, and Rangers (but with a big asterisk to be explained later) have their cap on a Hall of Fame member's plaque. And only the Brewers, with Paul Molitor and Robin Yount, have more than one.

In 1966, in just the second year of baseball's amateur draft—designed to help struggling teams land top talent—the Mets had the first overall pick. Mostly everyone in baseball had pegged the two top amateur prospects: a high school catcher from California named Steve Chilcott and a dynamic outfielder at Arizona State named Reggie Jackson.

But based on some questions about Jackson's character (there were whisperings that he was kind of cocky) and a personal scouting report from Casey Stengel, the spring after he retired as the team's manager, the Mets put their money on Chilcott. Jackson went to the A's, who had the second overall selection.

Jackson's rise to stardom was only rivaled by his self-confidence. A year after he was drafted by the Athletics he was out of the minors and up with the big club. By 1969 he was a bona fide star, slugging 47 home runs in Oakland. That was also the year that Jackson made the first of fourteen appearances in the All-Star Game. And, of course, in 1993, after two World Series MVPs and 563 home runs, Jackson was enshrined in the hallowed halls of Cooperstown.

Steve Chilcott, on the other hand, never made it out of the minor leagues. After six uneventful seasons of trying to make it to the majors, an injury forced him from baseball. Chilcott and Brien Taylor, selected by the Yankees in 1991, are the only number one overall picks no longer playing who never made it to a big-league lineup.

One future Hall of Famer the Mets did scout correctly was fireballer Nolan Ryan. In 1965 he signed with the club right out of high school. By the next season he was in the majors as the league's second-youngest player. Control problems plagued Ryan early on in his career, but by 1970 he seemed ready for stardom, tying a team record with 15 strikeouts in an April start against the Phillies.

But for some reason the Mets never trusted him with a full-time job in the rotation, which Ryan openly criticized. On December 10, 1971—because, as manager Gil Hodges said, "The Angels wanted him"—the Mets sent Ryan and three other players to California for shortstop Jim Fregosi.

Hodges further justified the deal by declaring, "I would not hesitate making a trade for somebody who might help us right now, and Fregosi is such a guy."

Fregosi had been to six All-Star Games as an Angel, but that was at shortstop, where his lack of offensive production wasn't such a problem. The Mets moved him to third base, and his first year's paltry .232 batting average with just 5 home runs became a major liability. It's also why that first season in New York was his only full season in New York. Midway through the 1973 season he was traded to the Rangers.

Ironically it is a Rangers cap that Ryan, with his 324 wins and 5,714 strikeouts, wears on his Hall of Fame plaque.

Closing out the trifecta of bumbled barters was the Mets' decision to trade Tom Seaver in 1977. In the cases of Reggie Jackson, who was still an unproven talent on the major-league level, and Nolan Ryan, who early in his career struggled with the strike zone, the

Mets can be given a small amount of leeway. History's hindsight has proven both moves horrible. But at the time you could make a small if unconvincing argument that the Mets were in the right.

In the case of Tom Seaver, however, New York knew what they had. Seaver had won the Cy Young Award in 1969, 1973, and 1975. From the time he was a rookie in 1967 until he was traded by the Mets a decade later, Seaver had finished in the top 10 in wins every season but two. And he also won three ERA titles and five strikeout crowns.

Simply put, Seaver was the best right-handed pitcher in the National League and in the middle of a sure-thing Hall of Fame career. Yet New York still chose to give him to another team.

In 1977 Mets chairman M. Donald Grant felt that Seaver had become greedy. Free agency was in full bloom in '77, and "Tom Terrific" wanted a redone contract that reflected the new rising salaries in baseball. That didn't sit well with Grant, a "word is your bond kind of guy," as described by his son, Michael Grant Jr. On June 15 Grant sent Seaver to the Reds in exchange for Pat Zachry, Steve Henderson, Doug Flynn, and Dan Norman.

In shades of *Butch Cassidy and the Sundance Kid*, incredulous Mets fan were asking the next morning, "Who are these guys?" New York sports reporters dubbed the trade "the Midnight Massacre." The spirit of a rabid fan base that the Mets boasted was quickly broken by the deal. Attendance dipped, Grant was vilified, and Shea Stadium became known around the Big Apple as "Grant's Tomb."

"I cannot even go into my own seat, in my own stadium," Grant said after the trade. "I have become lower than the lowliest bum on the street." A statement that I imagine many of the bums sleeping in the shadow of Shea Stadium in the summer of 1977 could probably confirm.

For the record, Seaver did put on a Mets cap when he was inducted into the Hall of Fame in 1992. He is the Mets' only official Cooperstown representative.

Disco Demolition Night at Chicago's Comiskey Park goes from a friendly radio station promotion to a game-forfeiting fan riot faster than you can say "jive turkey." *(© Bettmann/Corbis)*

Disco Demolition Night
July 12, 1979—Tigers vs. White Sox

Ah, the 1970s: leisure suits, giant gold medallions dangling in front of inappropriately displayed hairy chests, collars the size of pterodactyl wings, and rocks as pets.

If you are one of the poor saps born in 1980 or later who missed out on *Mork & Mindy*, bell-bottoms, and the Atari 2600, then this brief trip down memory lane means absolutely nothing to you. You never put on a mood ring, worried about mixing Pop Rocks and soda, or learned all about English grammar and the intricate workings of the U.S. government to the tunes of *Schoolhouse Rock!*

I bet, however, that you know all about disco. You've seen the platform shoes, marveled at the dance moves that only the most movement-challenged of white guys would dare invent, and heard the lyrics where every third word is "shake," "boogie," or "booty."

But do you know about the day that disco officially died? Have you heard the story of the fateful July evening in Chicago when America officially ceased to be funky? When we went from mondo cool to totally square?

This isn't just a story about a baseball team's extremely ill-advised promotional gimmick to drum up attendance. No, it's a story of America and a country of far-out dudes and dudettes turning the page on an out-of-sight decade, and using explosives in a crowded ballpark to do so.

The roots of the promotion, and the tiny flapping butterfly wings from half a world away that would eventually cause this cataclysm, were actually planted two years earlier. Mike Veeck, son of Sox owner Bill Veeck (of I-once-hired-a-midget-to-pinch-hit fame), was the team's marketing director. In 1977, while he and some of his front-office coworkers sat around a bar following a successful disco dance competition promotion, someone threw out the suggestion that the team now needed to have an "anti-disco" promotion. "It sounded like a terrific idea at four in the morning in Miller's Pub," recalled Veeck.

But it wasn't until 1979, after local radio DJ Steve Dahl created his "disco sucks" campaign and started an army of listeners "dedicated to the eradication and elimination of the dreaded musical disease known as disco," that the White Sox would plan the promotion.

Prompted by Dahl and cohost Garry Meier's on-air scratching of listener-requested disco albums, finished off by an explosion sound effect and the 98.3 radio frequency of Dahl's station, WLUP, Veeck and the Sox had their promotion. Anyone who came to Comiskey Park with a disco record in tow would be charged 98 cents admission to the White Sox–Tigers July 12 doubleheader. And those records that had been collected would be thrown into a giant Dumpster, taken out to center field between games, and blown up by Dahl, the self-appointed general in the war on disco.

Having drawn 15,000 fans the night before, White Sox officials were hoping to draw enough disco haters to push their attendance beyond 20,000 for the twin bill with the Tigers. What they got instead was a standing-room-only crowd of 55,000 and another 20,000 fans stuck outside the gates, jonesing to join the party . . . literally. A very recognizable-smelling cloud of smoke was hanging above the field before the first game began, and it was obvious to everyone in attendance that these were not your typical baseball fans.

Then, as the action began, it became painfully clear, also literally, that there were quite a few records that hadn't been collected. They instead were being flung around the stadium like sharp vinyl Frisbees, minus the willing participant on the receiving end.

That was followed by projectile cherry bombs.

Then beer cups.

Then anything heavy enough to fly through the air and leave a mark on its random target.

And then it was time to blow up the records.

Coming onto the field in a jeep and wearing fatigues and a helmet was "the general." Dahl took the microphone, began to fire up the crowd—who by this time was already nearing a frenzy—and then the bomb blew, sending album shards skyrocketing into the Chicago sky while simultaneously tearing a giant hole in the outfield grass.

And that was all she wrote.

Thousands of fans poured over the walls and onto the field, enveloping it like they were celebrating a World Series title. Bases were stolen. Numerous small fires were set on the field and in the stands. The batting cage was attacked and destroyed. The dugouts were looted of bats, balls, and helmets. Pandemonium ruled the night as the security staff on site ran to safety.

"I was shocked and amazed," said Dahl. "And I knew I was in trouble."

Owner Bill Veeck tried to plead with fans to stop the riot and clear the field. No one listened. Hall of Fame broadcaster Harry Caray got on the public address system to try and control the crowd. No one cared.

It finally took nearly forty minutes and thirty-nine arrests by the arriving Chicago police, complete with riot gear, before the field could be cleared of the unruliness. But by then it was clear that there would be no second game that night. The White Sox pleaded with the umpiring crew to let them continue with baseball. With a hole in the outfield (along with several other missing pieces of sod), smoldering debris still scattered about the playing surface, and a very real fear of the remaining Chicago fans, Tigers manager Sparky Anderson refused to have his team take the field for the second game. Umpire Dave Phillips called it a White Sox forfeit—a decision upheld by American League president Lee MacPhail the next day.

White Sox manager Don Kessinger said of the night, and the ruling, "We have found a lot of ways to lose games this year, but I guess we added a new wrinkle."

In an effort to save whatever face was possible with the rest of the baseball world, Mike Veeck was forced to resign (he has since been involved with several controversial minor-league team promotions, including free vasectomies during a Father's Day game). But the success of Veeck's promotion, hatched with anti-disco crusader Steve Dahl, was as noticeable as a 1970s Afro. Disco had been dealt a soon-to-be-fatal blow.

In all seriousness, the book *Rock of Ages: The Rolling Stone History of Rock & Roll* called Disco Demolition Night an "emblematic moment" of the rising tide of public opinion against disco.

And it points out that by the following year disco was on a very apparent nationwide commercial decline.

America's "disco fever" had finally broken.

The Stink of an Overfertilized Leaf
April 18, 1998—NFL Draft

> You can go five to ten years without getting a chance to draft a quarterback like this.
> —**Bobby Beathard, Chargers general manager, 1998**

> I have never seen an athlete work harder at destroying himself and his career than this guy.
> —**Bobby Beathard, ex-Chargers general manager, 2000**

The "this guy" that Bobby Beathard was talking about in 2000 was, of course, Ryan Leaf. While technically Beathard was still the GM in San Diego in 2000, his "ex-" status was soon to come, and in no small part because of the deal he made to trade up and draft the can't-miss prospect that would lead the Chargers for a generation.

Heading into the draft, however, it was far from a sure thing that Leaf would fall to San Diego. Football experts were divided as to which of the superstars, Leaf from Washington State or Tennessee's Peyton Manning, would make the better pro. Manning was older, had the NFL-quarterback pedigree, and was thought to be more prepared to move to the next level. But Leaf had the physical tools, had incredible numbers during his junior season (he was a Heisman Trophy finalist), and was, in the words of *Sports Illustrated*'s Peter King, "cool and focused, never panicky."

It was the ultimate case of can't lose for San Diego—once

they traded with Arizona to move up from the third pick to the second. If the Colts, with the first pick, snatched Leaf, the Chargers would take Manning. But if Indianapolis decided to go with the son of Archie Manning, then the Pac-10 Offensive Player of the Year would stay on the West Coast.

Six of one, half a dozen of the other.

As it turned out, it was Leaf who fell to the Chargers at number two. The crew in San Diego couldn't have been more excited. He looked like a quarterback and sounded like one too. When Leaf first met the local media he was an instant hit, telling the cameras, "I'm looking forward to a fifteen-year career, a couple of trips to the Super Bowl, and a parade through downtown San Diego."

The trade that gave the Chargers the privilege of drafting Leaf—two first-round picks, a second-round pick, linebacker Patrick Sapp, and three-time Pro Bowl kick returner Eric Metcalf—almost seemed liked a bargain.

"I've known Peyton Manning for a long time and I really love the kid," said Chargers offensive coordinator June Jones. "But when I went and watched Ryan Leaf work out, he was impressive. I came away excited about coaching Ryan Leaf. He is going to be a franchise guy."

And for two glorious games of football he *was* a franchise guy. Leaf started the season, and his career, with two straight wins, becoming the first rookie quarterback since John Elway in 1983 to accomplish such a quick start. Sure, Leaf's numbers weren't the greatest—he averaged just 185 yards while throwing 2 interceptions to just 1 touchdown—but he was winning.

San Diegans could hardly wait to see what the future of their salient signal caller would hold.

They didn't have to. The next game, week 3 at Kansas City's Arrowhead Stadium, could have easily been a re-creation of Custer at Little Bighorn. Ryan Leaf threw 15 passes that Sunday afternoon. He completed exactly 1. That was 1 completion, 2 interceptions, 3 lost fumbles, and a grand total of 4 yards. San Diego lost.

The next week out, Leaf connected on 15 passes to his own players. But four times he connected with the Giants' defense. San Diego lost.

Week 5 and week 6 were also losses. And Leaf collected 4 more interceptions.

Before the carnage mercifully ended with Leaf landing on the bench to finish out the season, he had thrown 2 touchdown passes and 15 interceptions; his completion percentage was a hideous 45 percent, and his quarterback rating was an embarrassing 39. Any way you looked at it, Leaf had a terrible rookie campaign.

But being a bad rookie quarterback is not an exclusive club. Manning's Colts finished 3-13 that season after he threw 28 interceptions. And Elway won his first two games, but he finished his rookie season with twice as many interceptions as touchdowns.

But being bad was not Leaf's chief failing. Bad as a rookie not only can be forgiven, it's pretty much expected. However, along with being terrible on the field, he had turned into a colossal a-hole off it. There were numerous blowups at the media and confrontations with his teammates. Instead of working out and watching film, his off-days were spent taking overnighters to Las Vegas.

He is alleged to have lied about a hand injury so that he could get out of practice to play golf instead. And once, when he was supposed to be rehabilitating injuries to his shoulder and wrist, he was caught on videotape playing football on the beach.

After missing all of 1999 because of that shoulder injury, and playing nine more miserable games with the Chargers in 2000 (11 touchdowns, 18 interceptions, and a quarterback rating of 56.2), and when it became painfully clear that he would never turn into an NFL quarterback worthy of the $31.25 million contract he signed, San Diego finally cut its losses.

In three seasons with the Chargers, Leaf had won four games. He set the franchise back years—it wouldn't break .500 again until 2004—and worse, two of the draft picks that Arizona got from San Diego to acquire the right to draft him turned into Pro Bowl players (Corey Chavous in the second round in 1998 and David Boston in the first round in 1999).

Upon his release in San Diego, Leaf bounced to Tampa Bay, then Dallas, where he made three pretty terrible starts, and finally to Seattle. But before starting the 2002 training camp with the Seahawks, the then twenty-six-year-old abruptly retired.

Because of Ryan Leaf, Bobby Beathard is rarely remembered as the football genius who built seven Super Bowl teams during a four-decade career. He is instead the sometimes out-there surfer guy who traded up for, and then drafted, the NFL's biggest bust.

10,000 Lakes and One Huge Mistake
October 12, 1989—Cowboys and Vikings

In my head-to-head fantasy baseball league last season I had a huge lead in the waning days of July. My team was hitting well, pitching masterfully, and staying relatively healthy. The championship was mine, with everyone else just hoping to play their way into having the honor of losing to me in the World Series. Just in case any of the owners hadn't quite accepted their signed and sealed fate, I used our league message boards to remind them. Daily.

Then it happened. On July 31, just hours before the trading deadline, a bottom-dwelling also-ran in the other division decided that Johan Santana, *the* best pitcher in baseball, was taking up space in his weekly lineup.

So he traded Santana . . . to the only team in my division

who had the slightest of dreams that they might dethrone me. And the price charged for Santana, of the we-have-an-entire-room-in-our-mansion-dedicated-to-housing-Cy-Young-Awards Santana? A utility outfielder working on his third team.

We live in a cold and unjust world, my friends.

And this was fantasy baseball. It's right there in the name: fantasy. It's not real (although don't let any of the legions of Roto geeks currently holed up in their parents' basements, clutching copies of advanced scouting reports of every ballplayer in the Venezuelan Professional Baseball League, hear you say that). Imagine if such a lopsided power-shifting trade, or even one far more egregiously unfair and involving many more players, happened in real sports. People would probably still be talking about it twenty years later.

Yes. It has been two decades since the Minnesota Vikings single-handedly won three Super Bowls for the Dallas Cowboys by believing that in a sport with twenty-two starting players, one man could make a team; and that there was no paid price too high to land the services of the great and all-powerful Herschel Walker. He was, after all, the best running back in the history of the USFL.

He was also one of the greatest college football players of all time, and one of the best athletes in recent memory. He's a six-degree black belt in tae kwon do and was a 1992 Winter Olympian in the two-man bobsled. And to be fair, he did have three very good seasons with the Cowboys prior to Minnesota mortgaging their future for him.

But this is football, not basketball. One man is not a franchise. And Walker was a running back. The average shelf life of an NFL back is 2.57 years, and Walker was going to Minnesota with a lot of mileage already on his tires. He had 1,147 carries in three USFL seasons and another 818 rushing attempts with the Cowboys. A used Porsche is a very nice car. But you don't pay brand new Bentley prices for it, and that's exactly what Minnesota did.

For Walker (along with two third-round draft picks, a fifth, and a tenth), Vikings general manager Mike Lynn sent Dallas five players, including starting cornerback Issiac Holt, and eight conditional draft picks, including three first-rounders, three seconds, and a pair of thirds. With eighteen players or draft picks changing hands, it was the largest single trade in NFL history. And because of the aftermath, the most talked about.

Walker was decent with the Vikings, but not great. He topped out at 825 yards rushing in a single season, but he never came close to being a Pro Bowl performer with his new team, and by 1992, after forty-one starts in Minnesota, he was gone to Philadelphia.

And Walker never came close to putting the Vikings over the top and into the Super Bowl. In 1989, with Walker playing the final five games of the season in Minnesota, the team won the NFC Central but lost in the first round of the playoffs. But in 1990 and '91, with Walker as the team's full-time starting running back, the Vikings missed the playoffs and lost 18 of 32 games.

Meanwhile, in Dallas, the Cowboys had used their passel of picks to land cornerstones Emmitt Smith (eight Pro Bowls) and Darren Woodson (five Pro Bowls). In a package deal involving several of Minnesota's other picks, the Cowboys were able to trade up in 1991 and get Russell Maryland (a Pro Bowler in 1993).

By the 1992 season, the year that Walker left his failures behind in Minnesota for a fresh start in Philadelphia, the Cowboys were in the Super Bowl for the first time in fourteen years. Dallas would win three of the next four Super Bowls, while over that same stretch of years Minnesota would fail to win a single playoff game.

When Herschel Walker retired from football in 1997 he had amassed 8,225 rushing yards and 82 total touchdowns. Emmitt Smith retired with 18,335 rushing yards and 175 touchdowns.

"The Trade," as it is still known in the state of Minnesota, was a horribly lopsided deal that was akin to trading in your job as the general manager of an NFL team to take the reins of a new and destined to be wildly unpopular minor league known as the World League of American Football. Exactly what Lynn, the chief architect of the deal that made him the most unpopular man in Minnesota and the name Herschel Walker a four-letter word, did after the local backlash in Minnesota forced him from his job.

Eighteen months after destroying the Vikings and creating the Cowboys, Lynn, as the CEO and president of the WLAF, delivered the game ball to midfield for the league's opening kick-off between the Frankfurt Galaxy and the London Monarchs very dramatically via helicopter. And like the initial flash but ultimate failure that defined the Herschel Walker trade, at the end of season 1, under Lynn's guidance, the WLAF was $5 million in the hole.

The Boz
June 12, 1987—NFL Supplemental Draft

Like most, if not all, of the teams in the NFL, the Seattle Seahawks have traded away more than a couple of draft picks that they'd like to have back.

In 1977, in just their second season of existence, the Seahawks traded the number two overall pick to Dallas for the number fourteen overall pick and three second-round picks. Seattle actually made the most of its selections, picking solid football players who played for several years with the team. But that number two overall pick in '77 was used by Dallas to take Tony Dorsett.

In 1985 the Seahawks had perhaps one of the worst collective drafts in team history. The first six selections they made that year (the names don't matter because I promise you've never heard them) played a collective total of six career games with Seattle. You would think that in six picks the team might have accidentally selected a player with an NFL career in front of him. But in 1985, you would have been wrong.

And let's not get into the gory details of quarterbacks Dan McGwire (1991) and Rick Mirer (1993)—both selected with first-round picks. Neither QB was ever able to win more than seven games in any one season. McGwire only managed two touchdowns in the thirteen career games he appeared in.

But these picks all pale in comparison to the fanfare that followed Brian Bosworth into the Pacific Northwest in 1987. He was Dick Butkus, Ray Nitschke, and Vince Neil (of Mötley Crüe fame) all rolled into one. He was part football player, part superhero, and 100 percent entertainer. And the blessed circumstances that brought him to the football fans in Seattle were clearly ordained by the pigskin gods above.

Bosworth's supplemental draft eligibility was a fortuitous mix of him graduating a full year before his freshman class at Oklahoma but still having a year of NCAA football eligibility left with the Sooners, which allowed him to opt out of the NFL's regular April rookie draft, where he would have most likely been selected by Indianapolis.

But even then, with a 10-6 record the season before, Seattle had only a 1-in-37 chance that it would win the weighted draft lottery for the right to pick the limitless linebacker. Which is why, when the heavens parted to the clarion sound of cherubic cornets and the Seahawks magically won, Bosworth's warnings to them that he didn't want to play in Seattle fell on the deafened ears of collective aspiration.

The Seahawks proudly selected Bosworth with their unexpected top pick in the supplemental draft, shoring up the defensive side of the football for a generation of Seattle's "Twelfth Man."

Except . . . it didn't exactly turn out like they planned.

Bosworth certainly acted like a superstar. He refused to come to Seattle during contract negotiations and only signed after the team offered up the richest rookie contract in NFL history, making him the team's highest-paid player. And he sued the NFL, demanding that even though he was a linebacker, and thus limited by the league's uniform rules to a jersey number in the 50s, he be allowed to wear his college number, 44.

He lost.

It became apparent as the season wore on that he was also losing strength.

If you remember, Bosworth had to sit out the final game of his collegiate career, the 1987 Orange Bowl, because of a positive test for anabolic steroids. That led to his infamous tantrum at the NCAA, where he called them "National Communists Against Athletes." But it also led the rest of America to speculate that much of his strength and endurance on the field was artificially enhanced.

The NFL, however, has a much stricter drug-testing policy. Quite often a player who dominates in college with the help of steroids will find the going much tougher in the considerably cleaner (but not quite squeaky clean) pro game. But it was unclear if, or how much, this affected Bosworth.

That is, until Monday, November 30, 1987, when the gridiron showdown for which everyone had been salivating happened on the Seattle goal line. Bo Jackson, merely playing football as a hobby (he maintained that his full-time gig was as an outfielder for the Kansas City Royals), broke into the open, with only Bosworth standing between him and 6 points.

It was no contest. Bo blasted his way through the Boz, knocking him backward 3 yards and ending all talk that the Mohawked mouth was the second coming of Jack Lambert. Seemingly overnight, Bosworth went from a standout rookie player and personality to an overrated and overpaid hype machine.

It was the beginning of an end that would come after just two dozen disappointing professional football games. At the age of twenty-four Brian Bosworth was forced to retire because of a chronic shoulder injury that many speculated was the result of earlier steroid use.

He has since made more than a dozen films as an "action star" (which is getting pretty loose with the language, if you ask me), and just recently his box-office totals surpassed the $11 million he conned out of the Seahawks.

"The Incredible Bulk"
April 23, 1989—NFL Draft

Speaking of much-ballyhooed physical specimens that fell just a little bit short of their pro expectations, there was none bigger, literally, than the 6-foot-6, 315-pound Tony Mandarich. The only thing higher than Mandarich's metabolism (he famously appeared on *Late Show with David Letterman* toting several food trays filled with an example of his typical daily intact of 12,000 to 15,000 calories) were the RPMs on the propaganda machine that drove him up the NFL's draft rankings.

Twice before the draft he appeared on the cover of *Sports Illustrated,* which nicknamed him "the Incredible Bulk." *SI* also said of Mandarich, who was said to have run a 4.7-second 40-yard dash, "With his size, speed and attack-and-obliterate style of play, Mandarich has broken new ground for offensive linemen, as well as for the game of football as we know it."

And that was tame praise compared to what his college coaches at Michigan State had to say. "As a junior he could have started on any of our Super Bowl teams," said Spartan head coach George Perles, a defensive coach for the Steelers when they won four Super Bowls in the 1970s. (I wonder how Jon Kolb, the starter

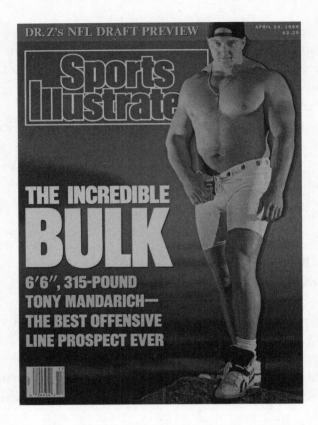

In a cover story published the week of the 1989 NFL draft, *Sports Illustrated* labels Michigan State's Tony Mandarich "the best offensive line prospect ever." But as the Green Bay Packers so painfully found out, he wasn't even close. *(Gregory Heisler/ Sports Illustrated/Getty Images)*

at left tackle for all four Super Bowls, and Gordon Gravelle, Ray Pinney, and Larry Brown, the men who held down right tackle, felt about a still-in-college Mandarich being deemed good enough to take their jobs.)

"He may be the best offensive tackle ever," continued Perles. "There's probably nobody faster in the world at his weight. This is a different player. We'll never have another."

But being the best offensive tackle ever was hardly the be-all and end-all for Mandarich. The man who was actually named to the All-Madden team before taking a snap in professional foot-ball (and this was twenty years before the current state of Mad-den's malfunctioning brain) planned on becoming Mr. Universe when his football-playing days were behind him. Mandarich told *SI* for its predraft cover story, "Why can't I do what Arnold [Schwarzenegger] did? Bodybuilding. Movies. All of it. I want to be Cyborg III."

It's interesting that he chose the word "cyborg" to describe the desired direction for his life. There were several in the Big Ten who were already convinced that he was far from nature-made. "We all know what's going on," said an assistant coach in the conference. "Pro scouts come in and ask me about Manda-rich. I tell them, but they don't care. It's really sad he's getting so much publicity."

One of the teams that didn't listen to the distant drumbeat of common sense and reason was the Green Bay Packers. With the second overall pick in the 1989 draft, right after Troy Aikman came off the board to the Cowboys, they selected Mandarich. He became the highest-drafted Canadian-born player in NFL history and an instant headache in Green Bay.

Mandarich, who had dropped out of Michigan State in March and moved out to Los Angeles, because, as he put it, "that's where all the things I want are—Hollywood, the weather, the beaches, the bodybuilding scene, the music," missed all of training camp in a contract dispute. (Note the conspicuous absence of football anywhere on his list.)

Finally on September 5, just five days before the regular sea-son started, Mandarich agreed to a contract that would pay him $4.4 million over four years. But it wasn't nearly the amount that he'd been seeking, and he was unhappy. Not surprisingly his head and his heart never showed up in Green Bay. It wasn't LA. There were no beaches or bodybuilders. It turned out that life as a professional football player is hard work, especially when there is much more regular drug testing.

Although Mandarich claims to this day that he never took steroids.

With Green Bay, the Incredible Bulk had the disposition of his comic book hero namesake, but never the strength or power. The guaranteed future Hall of Famer turned out to be extraordinarily ordinary. He was not Anthony Muñoz or Art Shell. He was Tony Mandarich, a run-of-the-mill NFL offensive tackle who spent three average seasons on the line in Green Bay. After he missed the entire 1992 season because of concussions and a thyroid condition (hmm, what injectable drug might cause that?), the Packers cut Mandarich before play began in 1993.

He did make a quiet return to football in 1996, playing three seasons with some really bad Indianapolis Colts teams. But after that he was done with football for good.

And not destined to become a movie star. Or Mr. Universe.

Instead, Tony Mandarich will always be judged by who he wasn't: the Best Offensive Lineman Ever.

The Plight of Sam Bowie
June 19, 1984—NBA Draft

The Tony Mandarich pick is also judged by the collection of future stars selected in the 1989 NFL draft immediately after he was taken second overall by Green Bay. Division rival Detroit nabbed Barry Sanders (ten Pro Bowls) with the third overall pick, Kansas City selected Derrick Thomas (nine Pro Bowls) with the fourth pick, and Atlanta got Deion Sanders (nine Pro Bowls) at number five.

What could have been in Green Bay, if only they'd heeded the warnings?

But there has never been, or conceivably ever will be, a bigger case of the "if onlys" than that which afflicts Portland Trail Blazer fans.

The disease was first noticed in 1984, when several Portlanders complained of a nervous tick at the idea that their beloved Blazers were putting their franchise's hopes on the legs of a man with a history of stress fractures, Sam Bowie. Over the next five years that tick developed into a debilitating stomach virus that caused severe bouts of nausea followed by long stretches of depression and malaise. Today, even though the cause of the illness is known to all, and the cure has taunted the locals in Oregon by their geographic proximity to Nike's headquarters in Beaverton, the condition is chronic. Blazer fans are destined to spend the rest of the lives as carriers burdened with protracted cases of Bowie-itis.

In 1984 new NBA commissioner David Stern first delivered the grim diagnosis on the USA Network's broadcast of the NBA draft: "Portland selects Sam Bowie, University of Kentucky."

Bob Cousy is credited with telling longtime and well-respected basketball scout Marty Blake, "Never take a flea if you can take a giant." And it is Blake whom Portland's general manager Stu Inman consulted about the merits of taking Sam Bowie. In Blake's words, "You get a great center once every twenty-two and a half years, so you better take advantage of it."

Of course, how often does a Michael Jordan come along?

The first and second picks that year came down to a coin flip between Houston and Portland. The winner of the flip would most assuredly take the guaranteed best pick, Hakeem Olajuwon. But the second pick was less certain in many minds. Not, however, in the mind of North Carolina coach Dean Smith, the man privileged enough to coach Jordan in college. He'd even called Rockets head coach Bill Fitch and told him that if he lost the toss, and lost out on Olajuwon, Jordan was the only way to go.

He apparently did not have the same conversation with Portland.

Bowie was a gliding, light on his feet 7-foot-1, 240 pounds. And before he'd ever even played a minute of college basketball, he'd been named a member of the United States Olympic basketball team in 1980. He was that good in high school. And he was that good at Kentucky—when he played. Bowie missed two full seasons because of stress fractures that were slow to heal.

But the Blazers had given him an extensive physical before drafting him. Al Albert, the lead broadcaster for the draft, even said, somewhat fatefully as it turned out, "There's no doubt he's recovered from those two years he sat out with stress fractures."

No doubt.

But there was also no doubt that Jordan contained franchise-changing talent in his 6-foot-6 frame. Albert said of Jordan, after the Bulls fell all over themselves to draft him with the third overall pick, "This man is a can't miss."

So we'll give Albert credit for a .500 batting average.

Michael Jordan was indeed a "can't miss." A can't miss that hit more true than anyone could have possibly imagined. There were other great stars in the NBA at time, like Larry Bird, Magic Johnson, and Julius Erving. But none of them changed the NBA or the way sports and sports promotion was thought of in the world at large like Jordan did.

And for Sam Bowie, it was the legs. In five seasons with the Blazers, Bowie averaged less than twenty-eight games played. After a complete rookie season in which he averaged a respectable 10 points and 8.6 rebounds, the stress fractures took over. He was never fully healthy again, and in 1989 he was finally shipped off to New Jersey along with a draft pick in a trade for Buck Williams.

That same season, Bowie's first with the Nets, Jordan won his fourth straight NBA scoring title. And the next year Jordan would win the first of six NBA Finals MVP awards.

Sam Bowie finished his ten-year NBA career with 5,564 points. Michael Jordan scored 32,292.

Sam Bowie was a solid, if never spectacular, basketball player. Not exactly what you hope for with the number two overall pick in a draft that turned out four future Hall of Famers—Olajuwon, Jordan, Charles Barkley, and John Stockton. But Sam Bowie was no Michael Jordan. And as unfair as it is, that's the standard he'll always be judged by.

When Irish Eyes Smiled
June 9, 1980—NBA Draft Eve, Celtics and Warriors

How many times have we seen an NBA team trade away a big man in an effort to stockpile more players, only to then watch that big man win a championship for someone else?

When the Bucks traded Kareem Abdul-Jabbar to the Lakers in 1975 it had been four years since Milwaukee had won a championship. That title drought has now stretched to nearly four decades, while Jabbar added five more rings to his trophy case in Los Angeles. The Bucks became repeat offenders when they traded away the rights to Dirk Nowitzki for Robert "Tractor" Traylor, Pat Garrity, and a draft pick. Just ask the Mavericks how that deal has worked out.

Inexplicably the San Francisco Warriors couldn't build a championship team around the most dominant player professional basketball has ever known, Wilt Chamberlain. So at the All-Star break in 1965 they traded him to the Philadelphia 76ers for three players and $150,000. Two years later the Warriors made it to the NBA Finals but lost . . . to Chamberlain and the Sixers.

Proving English philosopher and statesman Sir Francis Bacon wrong—the man some theorize to be the true author of what

Shakespeare wrote, "History makes people wise"—the Warriors also repeated their mistakes of the past and traded away yet another big man destined for the Hall of Fame, Robert Parish.

But trading away Parish in 1980 by himself wouldn't have been bad enough to garner special mention in this book of blatant bumbles. A swap of draft picks was included in the deal (the Warriors got the number one and the Celtics received the number three pick). Ultimately the trade became Parish and Kevin McHale (another future Hall of Famer) to the Celtics, for Joe Barry Carroll to the Warriors.

"There are three great players in tomorrow's draft," said Celtics president and general manager Red Auerbach, referring to Carroll, McHale, and Darrell Griffith, who was selected with the second pick by Utah. "With this trade we will wind up with one of them, plus Parish. We bought ourselves an experienced center, a guy who can get you 10 or 12 rebounds a night, can score, and is sixth or seventh in the league in blocked shots."

By trading for Parish and using the pick on McHale the Celtics also bought themselves the key to getting past the 76ers, whom Boston had just lost to in the Eastern Conference Finals. As head coach Bill Fitch explained at the time, "I've always been of the opinion that you aim to improve what has stopped you from going all the way. In our case that means Philadelphia and that big front line that includes Darryl Dawkins and Caldwell Jones."

Thanks to the Warriors and their generosity it was Boston that began the 1980–81 season with the best front line in the NBA, and perhaps of all time. Teaming with Parish, who made the first of nine consecutive All-Star appearances that season, and McHale, an All-Rookie first team performer and seven-time All-Star later in his career, was a guy who had just won the NBA's Rookie of the Year Award, Larry Bird.

Not surprisingly, with a threesome like that leading the way, the following postseason Boston avenged its loss to Philadelphia and went on to beat Houston for the NBA championship—the first of three banners that the "Big Three" would add to the rafters of Boston Garden.

To be fair to Golden State, Carroll was a big man. But he was a big man of unknown potential. In Robert Parish the Warriors had seen firsthand what they had. But they still traded him away in a misguided attempt to remake themselves into a championship team. That, of course, never happened.

And to be fair to Carroll, he wasn't a walking stiff. But he also wasn't the franchise player that the Warriors were hoping to land. He did play in one All-Star Game as a member of the team. But he also left them for a season in midcareer to play in Italy with Olimpia Milano. He returned to Golden State with an Italian league championship on his résumé, but with a loss of serious leadership cred. A committed teammate just doesn't leave the league for lire and lasagna four seasons into his career.

At least not one willing to sacrifice for an NBA title; and not one who will ever fare favorably in a comparison to the pair of future Hall of Famers who found their way to Boston in 1980.

The Broad Street Heist
June 20, 1992—Flyers and Nordiques

It's no exaggeration to say that in the history of Canadian junior hockey there has never been a prospect as highly touted as Eric Lindros. Not only was he a great goal scorer and offensive playmaker, he was a physical force who regularly dominated players five and six years his senior. He was dubbed "the Next One," a reference to Wayne Gretzky, known as "the Great One."

There were even some hockey pundits who thought that the

imposing physical presence of Lindros made him the more complete hockey player. As sacrilegious as it was, they even suggested that he would one day eclipse Gretzky as the greatest player that ever lived.

It's also no exaggeration to say that the single best move that the Quebec Nordiques/Colorado Avalanche made in the history of their franchise was to draft Lindros in 1991. Sure, considering the expectations, it sounds like a draft day no-brainer. But Lindros told the Nordiques prior to the draft that he didn't want to play in Quebec City, he didn't want to have to speak French, and if the team was pigheaded enough to draft him despite his demands that they not, he would never, ever, put on a Nordiques jersey.

Lindros was true to his word. At the draft, when Quebec made him the top pick taken, he refused to participate in the traditional donning of the team jersey. He also stuck to his word and never once laced up skates as a member of the traditional hockey doormat. Lindros held out the entire 1991–92 season, and for the fifth year in a row the Nordiques finished in last place.

It was starting to look like a terrible decision to draft Lindros. Not only were the Nordiques still bad, they looked foolish. They wasted a top pick on a guy who so hated their franchise that he was choosing no NHL career over an NHL career with them. That kind of a public humiliation doesn't exactly put fans in the seats and sponsorship money in your pockets.

Then in stepped the NHL. The Nordiques had taken the hard line with Lindros, refusing to trade him. But the league, extremely unhappy that their youngest and most talked about star was not on the ice, leaned on Quebec to give in and give up. More than a year after drafting Lindros they were finally "convinced" (strong-armed, actually, because as a financially impotent perennial cellar dweller they had zero muscle to resist the entirety of the NHL) to trade him.

Naturally, huge offers for the superstar-in-waiting came rolling in—and from places where Lindros could be both a marquee name and still speak his native English: New York and Philadelphia. But absolutely nothing surrounding Lindros's entry into the NHL could be easy. The trade, and both trade proposals, came with controversy.

As it was told by the Flyers, they had worked out a deal with Quebec that was set to be finalized, until the Nordiques abruptly backed out because of a new offer from the Rangers. Quebec, however, claimed that there was never a definitive deal with Philadelphia, and that their agreed-upon trading partner was New York. But ten days later, on June 30, arbitrator Lawrence Bertuzzi, after interviewing eleven witnesses and collecting more than four hundred pages of handwritten notes as to the series of events that went down on the morning of June 20, ruled that Nordiques president Marcel Aubut had indeed agreed to trade Lindros to Philadelphia eighty minutes before making the same agreement with the Rangers. In Bertuzzi's opinion a handshake was as good as a signature, and that meant that Lindros was headed to Philadelphia.

In exchange for the rights to negotiate a contract with the nineteen-year-old, Quebec received Ron Hextall, Chris Simon, Mike Ricci, Kerry Huffman, Steve Duchesne, a first-round pick in 1993, $15 million, and the rights to a Swedish teenager named Peter Forsberg.

It would turn out to be a haul of Stanley Cup proportions.

The next season the Nordiques completed the single biggest turnaround in NHL history. They went from the second worst record in hockey to the fourth best, making the playoffs for the first time in six years. And with the franchise's new higher profile and burgeoning value, the owners were able to sell the team to an ownership group in Denver.

The Avalanche was born.

By this time, the young Swede, Forsberg, was in the NHL and making a name for himself. He won the Calder Memorial

Trophy given to the league's rookie of the year, and would go on to play in seven All-Star games as a member of the Avs. The 1993 first-round pick included in the Lindros trade was used to select goaltender Jocelyn Thibault, who was in turn used by the Avalanche in the trade with Montreal that brought Patrick Roy to Colorado. When the Avalanche won their first Stanley Cup in 1996, no fewer than nine players on the team were directly or indirectly linked to the 1992 trade with Philadelphia.

There is simply no other way to look at the deal. It was Eric Lindros, and Eric Lindros alone, who was responsible for building the Stanley Cup championship team in Denver. Had the Nordiques listened to Lindros before the draft and passed on picking him, not only would there no be a Stanley Cup winner in Colorado, there might not be a hockey team.

Ironically, if the arbitrator had instead ruled in favor of the Rangers, sending Lindros to the Big Apple, New York would have given up Doug Weight, Tony Amonte, Alexei Kovalev, and John Vanbiesbrouck. And then it is very likely that the Rangers wouldn't have won the Stanley Cup in 1994, two years later. Kovalev was a key member of the Rangers' Cup-winning team. Amonte was used to trade for Brian Noonan and Stephane Matteau, who scored a pair of game-winning goals in the '94 playoffs. And Weight was traded for Esa Tikkanen, who was in turn packaged to St. Louis for Petr Nedved.

Clearly it was the best trade the Rangers never made.

As for the Flyers, who were deemed at the time the big winners on the 1992 Lindros sweepstakes, they made it to the Stanley Cup Finals once with Eric Lindros—a 1997 loss to the Detroit Red Wings. Compare that to Gretzky's six Stanley Cup appearances and four Cup titles.

"The Next One" also comes up more than 500 goals and nearly 2,000 points short of "the Great One" for their careers. "The Next One"? Try "the Not One."

DOA

April 18, 1995, and March 14, 1996—Canadian Football League Drafts

I'm as big a fan as there is of the 1989 film *Weekend at Bernie's*. It's a brilliant "dead guy becomes the life of the summer party as his corpse's presence keeps schmoes Richard and Larry alive" tour de force. And Terry Kiser's piercing portrayal of the lifeless Bernie Lomax keeps us on the edge of our seats and guessing until the very last dizzying plot twist.

Proving that when Hollywood properly mines its wealth of creative talent, lightning can indeed strike twice, four years later the nation was graced with another summer blockbuster, *Weekend at Bernie's II*. The voodoo curse on a man already dead was a pure stroke of genius. Writer and director Robert Klane hit the mother lode of imagination and inspiration. With no more cinematic mountains to scale, Klane no doubt retired to his inevitable legacy among history's great artistes.

But two years later, as if hatched from the brains of the countless struggling screenwriters populating every Starbucks within a two-mile radius of Sunset and La Brea in Los Angeles, the plot for *Bernie's III* was born. Bernie, still dead (of course), tires of his lavish lifestyle in the Hamptons and the occasional run-in with the Voodoo Queen of St. Thomas (you really need to see *Bernie's II*), so he heads to Canada to become a football star ready to lead his CFL team to the championship.

It's captivating in concept, genius in its cross-audience appeal (almost everyone is either a football fan or someday going to die), and you can print "Based on a True Story" across the bottom of each publicity poster.

That's right; this plot line is true. Sort of.

In 1995, after the Las Vegas Posse went belly up, the CFL had a special dispersal draft of the Posse's players still under contract. In the fourth round the Ottawa Rough Riders selected defensive end Derrell Robertson. Robertson played his college ball at

Mississippi State in the late 1980s and by all accounts had been a solid pro for the Posse. Ottawa was coming off a 4-14 season, so what did they have to lose? Perhaps Robertson could help them restore some credibility with their fans.

Or . . . not so much. You see, long before he was drafted it was a guaranteed certainty that Robertson was never going to report to Ottawa or play for the Rough Riders. He was dead. And he had been dead for five months, killed in a car accident on December 5, 1994.

"I don't know how it happened," Rough Riders coach Jim Gilstrap told the *Ottawa Sun*. "The league didn't know it until we told them. And we didn't know until a week ago when we couldn't find him."

Needless to say, a team that well organized in its player scouting wasn't long for the league. In 1996 the Rough Riders played their final game.

But because misery and humiliation love company, Ottawa was joined in football's hall of shame less than eleven months after they made Robertson the first dead-on-arrival draft pick, by the Montreal Alouettes. In the fifth round of the 1996 CFL college draft Montreal selected Northern Illinois defensive end James Eggink. When a football coach at Concordia University began looking over the Alouettes' draft selections, the name James Eggink prompted him to place a phone call to Montreal.

The coach clearly knew something the Alouettes did not. James Eggink had died three months earlier.

"It's an unfortunate situation but unfortunately neither we nor any other club knew what had happened," said CFL spokesman Jim Neish. "Even the school wasn't aware of it."

Alouettes owner Jim Speros called Eggink's family to apologize and said of the mistake, "I'm a little upset and embarrassed as an owner, no doubt. I'm not making excuses . . . but the research process can be very difficult."

So I ask you, and this question can go out to Jim Speros as

well: who is the bigger idiot? Is it Ottawa, the team that tilled this virgin soil of incompetence, so rich with the nutrients that make it perfect for growing the world's largest dunce cap? Or is Montreal, who saw Ottawa's shame the year before, and no doubt privately mocked them, but then followed them blindly off the steep cliff of stupidity?

It's a debate with no winners, just two enormous losers. Not unlike losers Richard and Larry, as played by Jonathan Silverman and Andrew McCarthy.

So there's the script! *Weekend at Bernie's Trois: Bernie Goes to Montréal.* Hands off, Starbucks hacks. This is my screenplay ticket to Hollywood fame and fortune.

ATHLETES

Every sports fan, young and old, has a favorite athlete, past or present. For me, it was and still is George Brett. As a young Kansas Little Leaguer the same summer that Brett won the MVP and made his historic 1980 run at .400, my eight-year-old self was powerless to prevent the developing fandom. He was my hero, and if the baseball fans in Kansas and Missouri had anything to say about it, he would have become our nation's president. When George Brett pulled on his familiar number 5 jersey, lathered himself in pine tar, and stepped between the foul lines, he could do no wrong.

Of course, that's not reality. In truth, Brett committed 292 career errors while grounding into 235 career double plays. He stranded base runners, struck out in clutch situations, and during the 1980 World Series he battled hemorrhoids. He wasn't Superman. He was human. Nothing says "mortal" quite like having to sit on an inflatable doughnut in the dugout to shelter your throbbing, tender vittles.

The fallibility of our athletic heroes has always been a part of sports, be it the interception thrown by Joe Montana or the missed birdie putt from Tiger Woods. But on occasion the mistake is of such a grand nature that it overshadows the rest of the athlete's accomplishments.

To be specific, I am only talking about blunders of the mind. Highlighting critical missed free throws or bobbled ground balls is pointless. These things happen with regularity and are such a part of all sports, they're ordinary. That is why in these pages you won't find indictments of Bill Buckner, Jackie Smith, or the most famous of exclusions, Fred Merkle. They committed errors of the body, which is nothing unique in sports.

These pages are instead about the head-scratching, choke-on-your-Budweiser, shout-at-the-TV, can't-believe-he-did-that, sudden-drop-in-IQ moments that leave us still, to this day, wondering, *what were they thinking?*

Live and Lett Die
January 31, 1993—Super Bowl XXVII, Bills vs. Cowboys

If, as James Joyce said, "Mistakes are the portals of discovery," then Leon Lett is the greatest American explorer since Lewis and Clark.

There are a number of great athletes who have unfortunately been branded by a moment of idiocy. One instant, out of a thousand, that forever changed the identity of their careers. But some athletes go above and beyond the call of stupidity—like Leon Lett, who served as the poster boy for total brain shutdown not once, but twice, and within ten months.

When the calendar ticked over to 1993, Lett was having the best time of his life. A seventh-round draft pick out of Emporia State, a small Division II college in eastern Kansas, Lett finished the '92 season, his second in the NFL, with 3½ sacks. He hadn't started any games for Dallas during the regular season, stuck

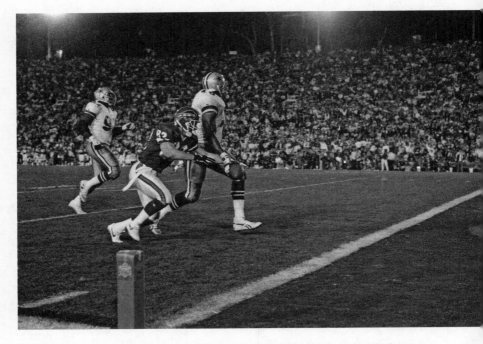

The Cowboys' Leon Lett showboats his way into Super Bowl infamy by turning a sure defensive touchdown into the forever definition of "never quit"—as defined by Bills wide receiver Don Beebe. Luckily for Lett almost no one watches the Super Bowl. (*John Biever/Sports Illustrated/Getty Images*)

behind defensive tackles Russell Maryland and Tony Casillas on the NFL's top-ranked defense, but the twenty-four-year-old had become a valuable member of the Cowboys' rotation along the defensive line.

For Dallas, the playoffs began with an easy 34–10 win over the Eagles. The following week, two days before Bill Clinton was to be sworn in as the forty-second president of the United States, the Cowboys advanced through San Francisco, 30–20, winning the NFC championship and claiming a spot in their first Super Bowl in fourteen seasons. Just three years removed from a franchise worst 1-15 record, America's Team was back.

Also back were the Buffalo Bills, returning to the Super Bowl for a record third straight time. They were 0-fer against the NFC East the previous two years, having lost to the Giants by the 2 feet of a missed Scott Norwood field goal, and to the Redskins, who dug a 24–0 hole that the Bills' "K-Gun" offense was incapable of climbing out. The Cowboys, with Troy Aikman, Michael Irvin, and Emmitt Smith, would provide the Bills' worst defeat yet.

Things started off poorly for the Cowboys. A 3-and-out, a blocked punt by Buffalo's Steve Tasker, and a quick four-play drive finished by a 2-yard Thurman Thomas touchdown plunge had the Bills off to an early 7–0 lead. After that, however, the Bills couldn't hold on to the football.

A Jim Kelly interception, followed by a Kelly fumble, led to two Dallas touchdowns. Then, in the second quarter, the next snap after the Cowboys scored their third touchdown—an Aikman to Irvin 19-yard touchdown pass—Lett stripped Thomas on a swing pass, giving the ball back to Dallas and setting up Irvin for his second touchdown catch in eighteen seconds.

The route was on, with everyone getting in on the act. By the time the Cowboys had pushed their late lead to 52–17, Leon Lett had a sack and two forced fumbles and was living every young defensive lineman's dream. A dream that seemed almost too good to be true when a Jim Jeffcoat sack forced yet another Buffalo fumble that bounced right to Lett with nothing but 64 yards of empty real estate between himself and a Super Bowl touchdown.

As things unfolded, it *was* too good to be true. Instead of Lett's name forever being etched into the Super Bowl record books, his dream turned to a nightmare, and he will forever be remembered as a Super Bowl laughingstock. Of the twenty-two players on the field, only twenty-one considered Lett's touchdown romp a foregone conclusion. The twenty-second man, Don Beebe, did not.

Squeezing out every drop of available speed, Beebe chased

Lett like a man possessed, erasing the 20-yard head start by the time the two players reached the goal line. Beebe's desperation sprint would have fallen short if not for the fact that of the twenty-one men who had already ruled touchdown, no one was surer of the six points than Leon Lett himself.

You play to the whistle, and you run all of the way to the goal line, but that's not what Lett did. He began to slow . . . and strut . . . and showboat . . . holding the ball loosely in his right hand and away from his body. The premature celebration was the final 2 yards that Beebe needed. Less than a yard away from Super Bowl immortality, Lett found infamy. Sprawling for the ball, Beebe knocked it cleanly from Lett's hand and through the back of the end zone for a touchback. Buffalo football.

Of course, on the scoreboard, the play was meaningless. The 52–17 score was the final margin of victory, and no amount of hotdogging was going to change that. But this was football's biggest stage. The paid attendance at the Rose Bowl was 98,374. Roughly 100 million Americans had tuned in to Dick Enberg and Bob Trumpy on NBC. And an estimated 750 million worldwide saw the game broadcast in their respective language. And every single one of them was laughing at Leon Lett.

Humiliation can't get more complete, can it?

Lett Bouncing Footballs Lie
Thanksgiving Day, November 25, 1993—Dolphins vs. Cowboys

Super Bowl Sunday has become America's unofficial national football holiday. But of the hybrid holidays that include an actual federal day off and a healthy helping of pigskin, no day is bigger than Thanksgiving. Among the heady credentials that Abraham Lincoln can crow about—preserving the Union and freeing the slaves—his creation of Thanksgiving has perhaps become a very close number three. If men were given the freedom to create a holiday from scratch, something very similar to Thanksgiving would most likely emerge. It's eating copious amounts of food, watching more than ten hours of football, and, somewhere in between, taking a nap. What's not to be thankful for?

Football fans owe their Thanksgiving traditions to Needham and Wellesley high schools in Massachusetts. In 1882 it was these two schools that played the first Thanksgiving Day football game—a tradition that the two have continued ever since.

When the NFL played its inaugural season in 1920 (it was known officially as the American Professional Football Association that first year), there were six games that Thanksgiving holiday. By the time the Detroit Lions joined the tradition in 1934, only three games were played. The distinction of a Thanksgiving Day NFL game was Detroit's alone from 1953 to 1965. In 1966 the Dallas Cowboys first played on the holiday. (The AFL played its own Thanksgiving Day games from 1960 until the merger with the NFL after the 1969 season.)

Sports celebrates its traditions like Homer Simpson does Duff Beer. There is a reverence given as if God himself had a hand in its creation. And because of that, and the national audience that always tunes in, everyone who plays in the NFL wants to play on Thanksgiving. They are the only people who actually want to work the holiday.

In 1993 the group of Cowboys employees were the defending Super Bowl champions. And with the rolling 8-2 Miami Dolphins coming to town for Dallas's annual Thanksgiving tilt, the hype going into the game was that the Dolphins and Cowboys could easily meet again in Super Bowl XXVIII. Come game time, however, the weather dominated the pregame talk and the pregame preparation. It was the coldest regular-season game ever played in Dallas, and the hole in the Texas Stadium roof, supposedly put there so God could watch his favorite team (so say the Cowboys), acted as an oversized ice chute for God to teach his favorite team about the phase transition of freezing water.

The field was covered in ice and snow from kickoff to the final improbable play. It was an ugly, nasty, turnover-plagued game, and a game that Leon Lett later called his best ever as a Cowboy. He also called it the "day [he] arrived in the NFL." He was dominating along the ice rink that was passing as the line of scrimmage, knocking down passes and harassing Dolphins quarterback Steve DeBerg whenever Miami needed a big play.

But the Cowboys' offense never truly got warmed up in the frigid Texas temperatures, and with just fifteen seconds left, Dolphins kicker Pete Stoyanovich, with his team trailing 14–13, lined up for a 41-yard potential game-winning field goal. However, he was only the *second* most important player on the field for that play.

The kick was blocked, and as the ball bounced helplessly toward the goal line the Cowboys' sideline erupted in celebration. But as he explained later, "I said to myself, 'Go get the ball'"; Lett didn't join in the merriment. He was, quite unnecessarily, passionately pursuing the rolling pigskin. Unnecessary because as long as no one touched it the ball would remain dead, giving possession to the Cowboys.

In the best of conditions, corralling a bouncing football resembles trying to snatch a skittish chicken. When the field is covered in ice and the footing has all the assuredness of a hike on Rollerblades up a landslide, it's like trying to catch that chicken while wearing boxing gloves.

Rocky Balboa might have pulled off the chicken chase, but Lett could not. As soon as he touched the ball, he fumbled it, making it live. And when the Dolphins' Jeff Dellenbach fell on it at the 1-yard line, Stoyanovich had a second chance with three ticks remaining on the clock. He didn't disappoint. The chip-shot kick was up and through, and the Dolphins had escaped Dallas with one of the most bizarre 16–14 wins in NFL history.

Just like Leon Lett's blunder ten months earlier, in the end it didn't matter. The Cowboys lost the game but won the war, repeating as Super Bowl champions with another win over the Buffalo Bills. And because of that fact, if the player who had inexplicably handed Miami the win had been anyone other than Leon Lett, the play would be long forgotten by now.

But this was Leon Lett, a specialist in nationally televised stupidity. If his Super Bowl gaffe branded him "King of the Boneheads," his Thanksgiving Day mistake tattooed the label in Helvetica Bold fully across his forehead.

During his very successful eleven-year pro career, Leon Lett won two Super Bowl rings and was twice named to the NFC's Pro Bowl team. But he is never thought of or referred to as Leon Lett, Pro Bowler. He is instead Leon Lett, pro punch line.

Miami Vice
January 30, 1999—The Night before Super Bowl XXXIII

Walk down the street for more than three minutes and you can be sure that you will have rubbed shoulders with one of the world's many dumb people. Dumb decisions, and the people who make them, are around us every day. There is a reason why the son of the president of Nigeria offers us $10,000 in money orders by e-mail almost daily. There are people who actually believe that for a comparably small fee the big money will be theirs. After all, he's the president's son. What's not to trust?

Why do you suppose irons now bear warning stickers that tell people not to use them on the clothes that they're wearing? Because someone actually did. And have you ever had the pleasure of spending a scintillating seven hours confined to a DMV-run traffic school? An afternoon there will have you wondering how we ever evolved through the Paleolithic period and advanced past stone tools. Or wondering if we ever did.

People do and say the dumbest things, and at the dumbest possible moments. A wedding-day toast is not the time to reminisce about all of the wild times in college you had as the groom's wingman. The Miss Teen USA pageant is the wrong place to show off your public school's geography program. And if you're playing in the Super Bowl, the night before the game is the wrong time to go cruising for a prostitute.

Through the years there have been plenty of players to party it up on Super Bowl Eve. The most famous of these is Max McGee, the aging backup wide receiver of the Green Bay Packers who imbibed one too many cocktails and three too many stewardesses (they wouldn't become "flight attendants" until 1978) during an all-nighter at Whiskey a Go Go just hours before the first Super Bowl was played in Los Angeles. However, it really didn't matter. McGee rarely played, catching only four passes all season long.

But on the third play from scrimmage starting wide receiver Boyd Dowler, in a moment of Wally Pipp-esque irony, separated his shoulder, thrusting McGee into the Los Angeles Coliseum spotlight hungover and sleep-deprived, and ultimately securing his spot in NFL history. McGee finished the game with 7 catches for 138 yards and 2 touchdowns, including the first ever TD scored in Super Bowl history.

What happened in Miami thirty-two years later, however, cannot be spun into a similar tale of colorful character meets serendipitous circumstance. Absolutely nothing good or fun came out of Pro Bowl safety Eugene Robinson's monumentally dumb decision and subsequent arrest on solicitation charges. Its aftermath was quite the opposite. The Falcons lost to the Broncos the next day and Robinson lost a Super Bowl–sized helping of dignity and respect.

According to the arresting officer's report, at 8:56 p.m. at the corner of Biscayne Boulevard and 22nd Street in Miami, Robinson pulled up to an undercover police officer in his rented Ford

Taurus and offered her $40 for oral sex. Upon learning that he would not be getting the hoped-for bang for his buck, and was instead a part of an undercover sting operation and headed for central booking, Robinson is alleged to have said, according to the report: "Lord Jesus, what do I tell my wife and kids? I am a born-again Christian. I have accepted the Lord as my Savior. I didn't mean to do it. I have disappointed my team, my coach, and my God. I was given the Bart Starr Man of the Year Award."

The Bart Starr Man of the Year Award that Robinson mentioned to the officer had been given to him just hours earlier by the Christian organization Athletes in Action. As decided by the players in the NFL, it is awarded to a person who displays "high moral character" and serves as a positive role model to his family, community, and team.

After getting bailed out of jail by general manager Harold Richardson, Robinson was joined in his hotel room for an all-night prayer session by teammates Cornelius Bennett, Ray Buchanan, and William White—all four of them starters forgoing sleep the night before the biggest game of their lives.

Head coach Dan Reeves, himself a devout Christian, insisted that the distraction of Robinson's arrest was minimal at most, deciding that his Pro Bowl–bound safety would still be in the starting lineup when his Falcons kicked off against the Broncos. But the idea that everyone was focused on football—Robinson even used the words "extremely focused" and "therapeutic"—was laughable. The play on the field simply didn't match the rhetoric.

Your wife or girlfriend can *say* that everything's fine. But even the dimmest of men can detect the truth behind her clipped responses and tightly pursed lips. Nothing is fine, and it's only going to get less so.

And that's what happened with the Falcons. Trailing Denver in the second quarter, 10–3, Broncos wide receiver Rod Smith beat Robinson deep for a game-turning 80-yard touchdown catch. Denver running back Terrell Davis was playing with a sore groin, and tight end Shannon Sharpe left the game with an injured knee. But Atlanta, with its solid defense and top ground attack led by Jamal Anderson, never did respond.

Blown blocking assignments and botched coverages in the secondary plagued the Falcons all game long. And according to the more honest players on the field, there was one unspeakable elephant-in-the-room reason.

"Instead of getting ready mentally for the Broncos, we were all talking about Eugene," admitted an anonymous Falcon. "The Broncos beat us, but anyone who says what happened to Eugene was not a factor is lying."

The familiar refrain coming out of Atlanta in the many days that followed Super Bowl XXXIII was that people make mistakes. In defense of his teammate and friend, Buchanan told a room full of reporters, "If anybody in here has never sinned, why don't you just raise your hand and let me know. We all fall short."

That's all well and good and true. But it's also hardly the point.

Robinson apologized at length to his team, his fans, and his family. He returned the Bart Starr Award (it was in turn awarded to 49ers tight end Brent Jones), and as part of a plea agreement he completed a diversion program, including an AIDS test and education class, which resulted in the misdemeanor solicitation charge being dropped. And for all of that he deserves to be forgiven. But his selfish act, and its disastrous consequences for his teammates, will never be forgotten.

Robinson doesn't get to be judged by the same standards as everyone else, because he chose to answer to higher ones. Part of who he was as a leader in the NFL was his morality. He chose to become the visible face of virtue in sports. And because he elevated himself with public prayers at midfield and repeated references to God when talking to the media, he had a much greater distance to fall.

It's simple. If you're afraid of heights, don't climb up the pedestal.

Eugene Robinson has no doubt paid for this Miami transgression and then some. But that doesn't change the facts, their consequences, or the ultimate end result.

Denver 34, Atlanta 19.

Safety Dance
October 25, 1964—Vikings vs. 49ers

California vehicle code violation 21651(b), otherwise known as "driving the wrong way on a divided highway"—a vehicle code far more relevant to the FOPH and FFBF (Friends of Paris Hilton and Famous for Being Famous) crowds—is a misdemeanor (above simple infraction but below felony) punishable by fines of up to $2,000 and jail time that can reach as long as one year. If someone is injured by your wrong-way drive, the violation becomes a felony, trading your jail time for some quality time in a state prison.

The potential prison time is on a sliding scale requisite to the kind of injury sustained, and whether in the process of committing said violation you are also engaged in other nefarious acts. The top of that scale is a life sentence, handed down in only the most specific of situations. The wrong-way trip must have happened in a very small, and now nonexistent, part of San Francisco, while the injury suffered is nothing more than a self-inflicted 2-point penalty in a football game.

Thus far the only violator, and only man forced to carry out this life sentence, is should-be Hall of Famer Jim Marshall, a man who defined everything a football player was in the 1960s and '70s. And a man who incredibly never missed a game during his twenty-year NFL career.

Officially Marshall is no longer in the record books as the NFL's version of Cal Ripken. His iron-man streak was broken in 2005 by punter Jeff Feagles. But Marshall played in the trenches as a defensive end in an era when cheap shots along the line were the norm, and he never missed a game. Whereas Feagles, with his wimpy kick-me kicker's face mask, was a player called on to appear in six or seven plays a game at most, and who was never called on to hit anyone.

Jim Marshall is the NFL's true iron man. If anyone deserves enshrinement in Canton, Ohio, it's him. Marshall also deserves a pardon from the life sentence that he's been serving since the moving violation he committed in 1964 inside San Francisco's Kezar Stadium.

In 1964, the first of four career All-Pro seasons for Marshall, the Vikings were still several years away from the string of 1970s Super Bowl appearances. But their "Purple People Eater" defense was already roaming the field. From 1962 to 1973 the Vikings ranked in the NFL's top 5 in either points or yards allowed in every year but two. And in those two "off" years—'65 and '67—their bruising defense ranked seventh and sixth.

Meanwhile Minnesota's opponent on that infamous October Sunday was the San Francisco 49ers, limping their way to a 4-10 last-place finish. Thus, absolutely no one was surprised that midway through the fourth quarter, on the back of a sack and forced fumble by Marshall that was scooped up by Carl Eller and returned for a Minnesota touchdown, the Vikings led 27–17.

That's where the score stood at the 8:12 mark, when 49ers quarterback George Mira hit Billy Kilmer (the future Pro Bowl quarterback wouldn't become a full-time signal caller until 1967) across the middle on a short completion. Just after Kilmer secured the catch, he fumbled, and with the loose ball bouncing near the line of scrimmage and a sea of empty green in front of him, Marshall began thinking about scoring his own defensive touchdown.

"I picked it up and started running," Marshall remembered. "Everyone was waving and shouting. I thought they were cheering me on."

They were not cheering, however. They were witnessing the unimaginable—and a play that in 1994 was ranked by NFL Films as the number one "greatest folly" of all time. The "folly," as it unfolded, is best described by the man who called the game that day, Lon Simmons:

> *Mira, straight back to pass . . . looking, now stops, throws . . . completes it to Kilmer up at the 30-yard line, Kilmer driving for the first down, loses the football . . . it is picked up by Jim Marshall, who is running the wrong way! Marshall is running the wrong way! And he's running it into the end zone the wrong way, thinks he has scored a touchdown! He has scored a safety!*

Upon completing his 66-yard uncontested romp into the wrong end zone, Marshall gave the ball a celebratory underhanded toss into the stands, completing the safety and giving 2 points to the hometown 49ers.

"What alerted me that something was wrong was the noise," said Marshall. "I had never heard a crowd react that way. Then I turned and saw some of my teammates pointing back the other way." And when 49ers center Bruce Bosley ran up to Marshall and said, "Thanks, Jim," the reality of his mistake landed like a ton of bricks.

Minnesota would hold on to win the game, 27–22, making Marshall the only injured party to emerge from Kezar Stadium. But his were injuries stretched wide open and prone to lots of pouring salt.

In the years to come, when the Vikings were on the road and leading, the other team's fans would often shout, "Give the ball to Jim. He'll score for us." And almost anytime he encountered an uninviting fan off the field, during his career and well after it was over, the irritating interrogation began. *Tell me about the play. Did you feel stupid? What were you thinking?*

Marshall has honed his answer over the years, explaining, "Think of the worst thing you've ever done—the thing you're most ashamed of—and it was seen by 80 million people. Then think of people coming up to you and reminding you of it for the rest of your life. That gives you a sense of what I've gone through."

At Ohio State Jim Marshall won two national championships. And in one game against Purdue he actually scored every point in a 14–0 win—scoring touchdowns on an interception and fumble recovery and kicking both extra points. During his twenty-year NFL career Marshall played in four Super Bowls, was an All-Pro four times, and is unofficially credited by the Vikings with 127 sacks. And to keep his 282-game consecutive streak alive (302 games when you include the postseason) Marshall twice left the hospital where he was being treated for pneumonia and ulcers, and once he played a game after accidentally shooting himself while cleaning his shotgun.

Yet even though his football résumé runneth over with the remarkable, one play defines his career. Subdued and philosophical, Marshall is resigned to his fate: "It's a helluva thing to be known for, isn't it?"

It sure is.

Wrong Way Roy
January 1, 1929—Rose Bowl, Georgia Tech vs. California

Jim Marshall's mental lapse in direction wasn't the first time a football player had shown a lack of orienteering skills. In 1938 the Washington Redskins' Andy Farkas scored the opening points . . . for Detroit . . . when he ran the ball to the wrong end zone for a safety. He ended up redeeming himself by scoring the lone touchdown in Washington's eventual 7–5 victory.

In a 1947 All-American Football Conference game between the Baltimore Colts and Brooklyn Dodgers, the Dodgers' right guard, Harry Buffington, picked up a fumbled football and began rumbling toward the end zone, only to realize just short of the goal line that he had run the wrong way. Buffington, in an attempt to pitch the ball to a teammate, fumbled it into his own end zone, where it was recovered for a touchdown by the Colts' Jim Castiglia. Baltimore went on to win, 16–7.

And then there is the case of Roy Riegels, perhaps the most infamous of the wrong-way runners and certainly the misdirected runner who had the most influence on sports history. The results and consequences of his compass confusion dogged Riegels the rest of his days. Like Jim Marshall, it became his life's legacy.

When the calendar turned over to 1929, college football dwarfed the NFL in both competitiveness and popularity. Red Grange appeared on the cover of *Time* magazine when he was starring at Illinois. But despite his enormous following among football fans across the nation, and the inroads Grange did make in popularizing professional football, the league he created, the American Football League, lasted just one season.

College football was king of the land, with fans far more committed to their alma maters than to the collection of professional football players who made, on average, less than $100 a game. And on January 1, 1929, all eyes of the college football world were on Pasadena's Rose Bowl. The slate of more than thirty postseason bowls that now dots the December and January calendars is a relatively new addition. In 1929 there was only one game in town. The Rose Bowl was created in 1902 as an East vs. West game that originally pitted a team from the Pacific Coast Conference (later the Pac-10) against a team from the eastern United States (the Big Ten didn't become the exclusive invitee until 1947).

With the game still scoreless in the second quarter, Georgia Tech running back John "Stumpy" Thomason fumbled on Tech's own 36-yard line. On one easy bounce California Bears center and linebacker Roy Riegels snared the loose ball, then got bumped, spun around, and then, suddenly finding himself clear of would-be Georgia Tech tacklers, took off in a sprint for the distant goal line . . . the wrong way.

As Charles Travers, then a Cal freshman, would recount to the *New York Times* many decades later, "You had to think quickly as to what took place. A lot of people didn't realize it was the wrong way."

One man, however, did notice. Without an ounce of hesitation Riegels's fleet-footed teammate Ben Lom immediately took off after the confused ball carrier. But as the two men neared each other, Riegels misunderstood Lom's shouted pleas as a request for Riegels to pitch him, the faster man, the football. Riegels, with a rarely encountered opportunity to score a touchdown in football's biggest game, naturally rebuffed Lom, keeping the ball and continuing his run. Finally, Lom succeeded in catching, convincing, and turning Riegels—just in time for him to get smothered by the pursuing Yellow Jackets at California's 1-yard line.

The times were different then, and the following decision by Cal coach Nibs Price is hard to understand in today's context, but on 1st down from his own 1-yard line, Price chose to punt. His team was shaken by the sudden shift in field position, and Price felt that the best way to stem the tide was by kicking the ball away. Turns out he was terribly wrong.

Placing the exclamation point on Riegels's wrong-way run, the punt was blocked out of the end zone by Tech's Vance Maree for a safety. Underlining Riegels's gaffe, those two points provided the final margin of victory in the 8–7 Georgia Tech win. And placing it in oversized bold italics, that win capped off a 10-0 season for the Yellow Jackets, giving them the national championship.

In describing to the Associated Press how things went so terribly wrong, Riegels explained, "I was running toward the sideline when I picked up the ball. I started to turn to my left, toward Tech's goal, when somebody shoved me, and I bounded right into a tackler. In pivoting to get away from him I completely lost my bearing."

But he found his way into the collective consciousness of generations of American football fans.

It is estimated that more than 450,000 column inches of newspaper space were written about Riegels's blunder in the days that followed, with some witty sportswriter wordsmith tagging him with the lifelong moniker "Wrong Way Riegels." Riegels quickly became a national joke, receiving numerous gag gifts, including upside-down cakes and train tickets that began at the end of the line.

Riegels would rebound from that disastrous day in Pasadena. The following season, as a team captain for the Bears, he was named to the AP's All-American team. Later he would become a member of the Cal coaching staff. He went on to serve in the Army Air Corps in World War II and was honored late in life by being named to both the Rose Bowl Hall of Fame and the University of California Hall of Fame.

Eventually he was able to develop a sense of humor about the misdirected notoriety that followed him the rest of his life. When Georgia Tech inducted its entire 1928 national championship team into its own Hall of Fame in 1971, Roy Riegels was there as a special invited guest.

As he received a personalized membership card to the Georgia Tech letterman's club, Riegels joked, "Believe me, I've earned this."

When a young player at Paramount High School in California intercepted a pass and then ran 55 yards to his own end zone for a safety, it was Roy Riegels who reached out to the dejected teenager, otherwise unknown to Riegels.

In a letter reprinted by the Associated Press, Riegels wrote:

For many years I've had to go along and laugh whenever my wrong way run was brought up, even though I've grown tired of listening and reading about it. But it certainly wasn't the most serious thing in the world. I regretted doing it, even as you do, but you'll get over it.

Just as Wrong Way Roy Riegels eventually did.

Tackling Dummy
January 1, 1954—Cotton Bowl, Alabama vs. Rice

Hollywood has always had a love affair with sports movies—some good, many bad, and even a few that realistically capture the essence and energy of the sport and its athletes.

In football, the excellent films include *Rudy*, *Brian's Song*, *Heaven Can Wait* (do yourself a favor and see it if you haven't), *Remember the Titans*, *Jerry Maguire*, and *The Longest Yard* (the Burt Reynolds original). The "misses" list is headlined by *Necessary Roughness* (just typing the title makes me angry), *The Replacements* (Keanu Reeves . . . enough said), *Johnny Be Good* (Anthony Michael Hall as a star quarterback . . . enough said), and the farcical and sanctimonious *The Program*.

I know a lot of would-be football cinephiles claim *The Program* is one of the better sports films. But if you place yourself among those ranks, you are wrong. It's written by David S. Ward, the writer of both *The Sting* and *Major League*. And the WGA rules on this are very clear, even though they remain unwritten. If you write arguably one of the best baseball movies ever and win an Oscar for writing what is inarguably one of the top-5 movies of all time, you are not allowed then to turn out something as ordinary and unimaginative as *The Program*.

It's almost as if Ward was engaged in a cliché-off with *Blue*

Chips writer Ron Shelton, who took his dip in originality after writing *Bull Durham* and *White Men Can't Jump*.

You have the alcoholic quarterback, the girl who swears that she'll never date a football player only to fall in love with one (the obligatory ironic twist), the coach who has one last chance to field a winner, and, of course, the obligatory valuable lesson about life, love, and how there is no "I" in team. And let's not forget the steroid use that prompts defensive star Steve Lattimer to celebrate his ascension to the first team by putting his head purposefully through the windows of several parked cars.

It's what every coach wants, right? A defensive player who wants to tackle anything that moves, even when it's parked.

In most cases, yes. Commentator Heywood Hale Broun said, "Football is, after all, a wonderful way to get rid of your aggressions without having to go to jail for it." And it's that attitude that makes a defensive player. But on occasion the enthusiasm for the tackle and the conviction of contact can get away from a zealous young player. Sometimes instead of the tackle eliciting "atta boys" from his position coach during Monday's film session, it leads to a lifetime of ridicule and mockery from the masses.

You probably don't know the name Tommy Lewis. Even many of the most knowledgeable college football fans can't place the name with the face. But I'd be willing to bet a collector's edition DVD of *The Garbage Picking Field Goal Kicking Philadelphia Phenomenon*—autographed by Tony Danza, no less—that you've seen Tommy Lewis's most famous, although far from proudest, moment.

It was the first day of 1954, and Rice's Dicky Moegle (he later changed the spelling to Maegle, as it's pronounced) was on his way to 265 yards rushing—a Cotton Bowl record that would stand for fifty-four years. On the strength of Moegle's legs, the Rice Owls beat Alabama, 28–6, and finished their Southwest Conference cochampionship season with a 9-2 record. But by January 2, 1954, all of that was forgotten or ignored.

In the second quarter, with Rice leading 7–6 but backed up at its own 5-yard line, Moegle broke free of the Alabama defense at the line of scrimmage and appeared to be on his way to a 95-yard touchdown run. But just after crossing midfield near the Crimson Tide sideline, Moegle was brought down with a touchdown-saving tackle by Tommy Lewis.

For a moment, nobody spoke or moved. The crowd went silent and the game announcers went mute. Everyone wondered, where did Lewis come from? And why isn't he wearing a helmet?

Then confusion turned to cognition, which then turned to utter and total disbelief. Lewis wasn't wearing a helmet because he'd come from the Alabama sideline. Lewis wasn't wearing a helmet because he wasn't in the game. In fact, he was a fullback, and the man who had scored Alabama's six points in the first quarter.

"I kept telling myself, 'I didn't do it. I didn't do it.' But I knew I had," recalled Lewis. And the crushing weight of that embarrassing reality wrecked Lewis for the rest of the game.

Moegle was awarded the 95-yard touchdown that he would have scored, and as the two teams ran off the field at halftime, Lewis jogged over to Moegle and threw his arm around him for the second time that day.

"At first I thought it was one of my teammates," said Moegle. "He had tears streaming down his face. He apologized and apologized, and he said, 'I don't know what got into me. I hope they don't string me up on these goalposts.'"

Two days later, while appearing on *The Ed Sullivan Show*, Lewis had an answer to the question everyone, including himself, was asking: why? Lewis replied famously, "Mr. Sullivan, I guess I was just so full of Alabama."

Sullivan played up the line and Lewis, leaving Moegle to feel like he was the heel and Lewis was the hero. And because he was Ed Sullivan, the rest of the media followed suit. In its weekly sports roundup, *Time* magazine, under the title "Alabama's

In perhaps the most bizarre sequence of events ever recorded at a college football game, from the sideline Alabama's Tommy Lewis sizes up Rice running back Dicky Moegle (top), he dives onto the field to make the tackle (middle), and then prepares to head back to the bench to hide from officials (bottom). *(© Bettmann/ Corbis)*

Twelfth Man," gushed about Lewis, "under his crimson jersey there burns an impulsive pride of state and university."

Years later Lewis revealed that he was actually full of something else. The "full of Alabama" line, the line that got him applause at *The Ed Sullivan Show* and a glowing write-up in *Time*, had in fact been fed to him by Sullivan.

The irony of it all was that Lewis wanted none of it. He wanted the play, the notoriety, and his growing status as a folk hero to all go away. "I'm reminded of the play frequently," Lewis told the *San Antonio Express-News* in 2006. "But anyone who knows me, and all my old teammates, would never bring it up. They know that play devastated me, and I have to live with it."

As the most bizarrely famous play in the history of college football, it will always live on.

This Is Your Brain on Drugs. Any Questions?
July 3, 2003—Tucson Airport

There are a few things in this world that will always remain a mystery to me. They are enduring riddles that defy everything that I, as a rational and educated human being with a cursory understanding of our physical and emotional worlds, know to be true.

Like, why is it that when I heat up a bowl of refrigerated day-old spaghetti in the microwave for five minutes, I can never get the center warm; yet when cooking a frozen Hot Pocket for the directed one minute and thirty seconds, the cheese comes out three times hotter than the surface of the sun? Why do all cars, regardless of make, model, or year, put the steering wheel, gas pedal, and brake in uniform locations, but leave us guessing as to the location of the gas tank? Or why over the years does a man's swimwear of choice grow proportionally smaller, while at the very same time his girth and volume of body hair inversely explode in expansion?

And then there is the mystery of mysteries. A puzzlement so perplexing that to try and explain it only accentuates the absurdity. I am, of course, talking about Damon Stoudamire's alleged decision to sneak marijuana past Tucson's airport security, and through the metal detector, by wrapping it in aluminum foil!

Forget for a moment that Stoudamire spent four years at the University of Arizona. Or that he was even deemed smart enough to get into what is considered an academically respected college. Or that, as a multiple marijuana offender and obvious cannabis connoisseur, guru of the ganja, and epicure of herb, over the years he must have used many discreet methods of transportation that do not involve shiny metal.

Doesn't he own a microwave?

Every six-year-old with access to this decades-old invention understands the metallic properties of foil. Anyone who has ever flown on a commercial airliner—which most certainly includes the frequent fliers of the NBA—has seen those very properties result in many a passenger getting hand searched by the men and women of the TSA. And even though, as of yet, no one has successfully hijacked an airplane with a baggy full of buds (the infamous "Demand for Doritos" incident on a 1998 Southwest Airlines flight from Las Vegas notwithstanding), they're not likely to give your grass a pass, even if you are a famous basketball player.

Predictably, at least to most people with functioning neurons, Stoudamire set off the metal detector as he prepared to board a flight to New Orleans. (New Orleans over the July 4 weekend. You couldn't just buy some there?) And after he emptied his pockets and placed both the foil-wrapped pot and a package of rolling papers into a plastic security bin, the police were summoned. Predictably, when the police discovered the nearly 40 grams of weed (about 1½ ounces), they arrested Stoudamire and charged him with possession of marijuana and possession of drug paraphernalia, both misdemeanors.

Since this wasn't exactly the former "Jail Blazer's" first time at the rodeo, when word of the arrest reached Portland, the team immediately fined the dope of dope $250,000 and suspended him for three months. The previous November, while driving back to Portland after a game in Seattle, Stoudamire and teammate Rasheed Wallace had been charged with possession of marijuana when the car they were in was pulled over for speeding. And the February before that, this devotee of doob was charged with felony possession of marijuana when police, while responding to a burglar alarm at Stoudamire's house, discovered more than 150 grams of the drug. That charge was later dropped when a judge ruled the search illegal because the police were there only to respond to the alarm.

Other than being lighter in the wallet and even more sullied in the eyes of his fans—as if that was possible by that point—Stoudamire once again dodged the reefer bullet. It took some legal doing, and more than a little of his own green (the legal tender kind), but nearly five years later, after two appeals to the Arizona Supreme Court, Stoudamire's attorneys got the charges stemming from his airport arrest dropped.

Stoudamire paid no fine, other than to his team. And he never served a day in jail. But on that day at the Tucson airport, Stoudamire put on a permanent dunce cap of shame that can never be removed.

So for all of you harbingers of hemp who refuse to believe that excessive marijuana use does in fact kill brain cells, let the cautionary tale of Damon Stoudamire and the functioning metal detector serve as your warning.

C-Webb's TO

April 5, 1993—Final Four, North Carolina vs. Michigan

As was first noted in the Old Testament book of Ecclesiastes, and then later put to the drug-inspired music of the 1960s, there is a time for everything. A time to be born, and a time to die. A time to love, and a time to hate. A time to laugh, and a time to weep. A time to get, and (most certainly) a time to lose.

Failing to make the editor's final cut in both Ecclesiastes and Pete Seeger's folk lyrics, as performed most famously by The Byrds, is "a time to call timeout, and a time to let play continue." But there is a season for the ostensible contradictions of "time" and "timeout." That season is spring, when the madness of March flips the calendar to the Final Four frenzy of early April.

It is more than a little ironic that as we increasingly become a spank-free society insistent that the "timeout" is a kinder, gentler, and less-damaging form of childhood punishment, the timeout called by young basketball star Chris Webber in the 1993 NCAA championship game, and the pain it caused, has continued to deepen its scars. Despite a pro career that featured five NBA All-Star Game appearances, Webber will always be remembered as the recently turned twenty-year-old calling the deer-in-the-headlights timeout to seal his Final Four fate.

There has never been a group of college basketball players more celebrated than the University of Michigan's freshman class of 1991. When April of 1993 rolled around and the Fab Five (Webber, Jalen Rose, Juwan Howard, Jimmy King, and Ray Jackson) were making their second straight trip to the finals of the Final Four, it looked like there might not be any group that was better. As super-sophs the fivesome was a year older, an NCAA Division I season wiser, and a good bet to beat Dean Smith's North Carolina Tar Heels to win the national championship.

Throughout most of the contest Michigan was in control, leading 67–63 with just 4:31 to play. But the game, the momentum, and history began to change when the Heels' Donald Williams drained a 3-pointer to narrow the lead to 1. It was the beginning of a comeback that has largely been forgotten because of the game's final events—the four and a half minutes of great basketball for which North Carolina has never fully received the credit it deserves.

Jalen Rose tried to answer for Michigan but failed on the shot. Back at the other end Derrick Phelps scored to give Carolina a 68–67 lead. That was followed by another Rose miss and another basket for the Heels, with George Lynch extending the lead to three.

After another Michigan turnover and an easy two for Eric Montross to put UNC up 72–67, Ray Jackson was able to arrest some of the Carolina blue tide with a jumper that pulled the Wolverines back to within three. Then, with just forty-six seconds to play, Michigan coach Steve Fisher decided to call his team's final timeout.

Breaking the huddle, Fisher shouted to his team, "No more timeouts." The warning is standard procedure for a coaching staff after they've used their final clock stoppage, and it's done in every single basketball game at every single level of play. There is no doubt by anyone on or near the Michigan bench that Fisher and his staff made sure that the five Wolverines who took the floor for the final forty-six seconds of the season knew that they were out of timeouts.

Or, at the very minimum, they were told. Hearing is an entirely different matter.

As it turned out, the timeout was perfect. On the inbounds pass Michigan forced the turnover, and on a putback from another Rose miss, Webber scored to cut the Carolina lead to 72–71. Then, on the following Heels possession, Pat Sullivan was fouled. After making the first of his two free throws, Sullivan missed the second off to the left, with the rebound and a last-second chance to tie or win kicking straight to Webber and his Wolverines.

And that is when things got historic.

With Webber securing the ball directly in front of the North Carolina bench, the rest of the players on the floor retreated to the other end, leaving the 6-foot-9 center to bring the ball up the floor alone. Unsure of what to do—dribble the ball or instinctually call a timeout—Webber did a hybrid of both and traveled in the process.

The North Carolina bench erupted, waiting for the call that would return them possession of the ball. But with no whistle, Webber moved up the floor and across mid-court. Then, still without help from his better-ball-handling guards, and now squarely in the middle of uncomfortable defensive pressure from Lynch and Phelps, Webber did the only thing he could think of: he called timeout.

And there was your ball game.

On the resulting technical foul Williams made both free throws. The ball then was inbounded to Williams, who was quickly fouled. And with two more made free throws North Carolina had its 77–71 win and head coach Dean Smith had his second national championship—both coming at the Superdome in New Orleans and both, ironically, coming with major last-second assists from his opponent. (In 1982 Georgetown's Fred Brown passed the ball directly to James Worthy, salting away the championship for UNC and making Michael Jordan a legendary championship-winning shot maker.)

No one wanted to make a timeless goat out of the young and talented Webber. When Webber first started to call the timeout and ended up traveling instead, referee Jim Stupin says that he intentionally turned away from Webber. Stupin recognized what Webber was about to do, and he didn't want to have to call a technical foul on the twenty-year-old for taking the extra time-out. Stupin's thinking was, *If I don't see it, I can't call it.* And in his effort to protect Webber, Stupin missed both the aborted time-out call and the traveling violation.

Of course, when Webber very demonstrably called the time-out moments later in front of the packed house at the Superdome and millions of national television viewers, it was impossible to ignore and no longer possible for the referees to save Webber from himself and the unkind cut of history's judgment.

After the game a despondent Webber told reporters, "I just called the timeout and probably cost us the game."

It's hard to argue with Webber's very succinct analysis of the final seconds. If he didn't cost his team the game, he certainly cost them an opportunity to win it. Even his supporters, including both head coaches, couldn't muster up much of a defense. Steve Fisher said, "We thought we mentioned [we were out of timeouts]. Apparently we didn't make the point specific enough."

And Dean Smith feebly tried to get Webber off the hook by telling reporters, "I don't think that timeout necessarily cost Michigan the game."

Nice, but not true. It did.

However, years later, Webber did find a loophole in history that ultimately makes his timeout a moot point. Thanks to Webber's improper involvement with UM booster Ed Martin and Martin's rather large bank account (Martin had been giving Webber and his family money since Webber was in the eighth grade), Michigan has since forfeited all of its wins in the 1992 and 1993 NCAA tournaments and removed both Final Four banners from the rafters of Crisler Arena.

So now there are two entirely different reasons Michigan didn't win the 1993 national championship, and both of them are Webber's doing.

Old Man Beatdown
August 4, 1993—White Sox vs. Rangers

One of the most regrettable results of the continued American slide down the dark pit of political correctness, along with the wussificating trend of eliminating scorekeeping in youth sports because we never ever want to tell children they lost (don't we actually learn more from our defeats?), has been the elimination of brawls in sports. You may be afraid to publicly admit it, but you know you miss them.

In the NBA it's an automatic ejection and suspension if you leave the bench and join an on-court fracas, even if you never throw a punch. The NHL, in which fighting is as important as goal scoring, and in which players make careers out of being on-ice goons, strictly forbids clearing benches. And the next time you see a football fight in which something actually happens, it will be the first time. Maybe it's the excessive pads, the helmets and face masks, or the fact half of the team is made of up of lumbering 300-pounders, but football players like fighting about as much as they like Lean Cuisine.

And let's not waste our time addressing the aversion to fisticuffs that saturates the soccer world. These yahoos are too busy writhing on the field in the kind of agony that should only be reserved for farm equipment accidents and tire irons to the groin to actually go toe-to-toe with the opponent who ever so slightly nudged them off the ball.

But in one of the true ironic paradoxes in all of sports, baseball, a noncontact game played by men in tight knickers generally derided as sedentary nonathletes subsisting on jumbo bags of sunflower seeds and twelve-packs of Miller High Life, still brawls old-school style.

Sure, there are the ridiculous sprints into the infield by competing relief pitchers who would sooner nap in their bullpens than fight on the field. And when old fat guys like Don Zimmer decide to get into it with players half their age and half their body mass, it's more than a bit embarrassing. But with no padding and few helmets the baseball brawl remains a thing of beauty and one of our last links to a past time when men were allowed to settle things the way men, and third graders, were meant to: with fists, slaps, tackles, and the occasional flying karate kick.

We all have our favorites. There was 1965, when Giants pitcher Juan Marichal swung his bat upside the head of Dodgers catcher John Roseboro. In 1998 the Yankees' Darryl Strawberry got in one of the best punches ever thrown in a basebrawl when he clocked Orioles pitcher Armando Benitez. And in 2000 the Tigers and White Sox engaged in a pair of bench clears that left reliever Keith Foulke with five stitches in his face and twenty-five players, coaches, and managers fined or suspended.

My personal favorite (and judging by the number of views the video still gets on YouTube these many years later, one of the most celebrated baseball fights of all time) was the ill-advised charging of Nolan Ryan by Robin Ventura.

It's the most basic tenet of Sun-tzu's *The Art of War:*

If fighting is sure to result in victory, you must fight. If fighting will not result in victory, then you must not.

It could be the ignorance of youth. Ventura was only twenty-six at the time and coming off his first All-Star appearance in 1992. Ryan, on the other hand, was forty-six, in the final year of his career, slow, and aging. But when Ventura chose to rush Ryan after the Hall of Famer hit him in the arm with a 3rd-inning in-side pitch, it was perhaps the worst decision Ventura made in his sixteen major-league seasons.

Racing to the mound with his manhood to defend, all Ventura ended up doing was having it questioned by every baseball fan and sports talk radio host across the country. Instead of running away from the charging batter, Ryan took a step to his left, almost inviting the confrontation, and went on the offensive as soon as Ventura arrived. The old Texan rancher, in a move that he later claimed to have learned while subduing cattle, captured Ventura in a headlock with his left arm and began to pummel him without mercy with his right.

After six emasculating uppercuts to the head and face, Ventura was granted his reprieve when Ivan Rodriguez, Ryan's catcher and quickly conscripted protector of Ventura, separated the two like a boxing referee who had finally seen enough and was calling a TKO.

In a move of humanitarianism, the umpires ejected Ventura, sparing him the indignity of having to face the crowd for six more innings and having to step in again against the superior Ryan, who for his part was not ejected. And just in case there was any doubt after the confrontation was finished and the punishment was doled out who the superior player was, Ryan didn't allow another hit on the way to recording his 322nd career win.

Ryan explained afterward that despite appearances, he did not want to fight with Ventura: "If Robin would've come out there and stopped before he got to the mound, I wouldn't have attacked him. But when he came out and grabbed me, I had to react to the situation. That's what I try to tell people, but it looks like I used him for a punching dummy when people play the clip."

A clip that shows just why Ryan was such an intimidating force in baseball for nearly three decades, and one that will forever define the consequences of making an unthinking decision.

As Sun-tzu wrote:

Tactics without strategy is the noise before defeat.

If the Shoe Fits . . .
May 4, 1957—Kentucky Derby

If you've spent any time around athletes out of their sporting element (hotels, college classrooms, etc.), it's easy to pick them out from the regular Joes like you and me. They are big, they look strong and fit, and there is an athleticism that almost oozes from their pores. I had the privilege of shooting pool with Tony

Gallant Man and jockey Willie Shoemaker (5) get nipped at the wire of the 1957 Kentucky Derby by Iron Liege and Bill Hartack after Shoemaker mistakenly stands up in the saddle one pole too soon. *(© Bettmann/Corbis)*

Gonzalez while both of us were wearing his number 88 Kansas City Chiefs jersey. And to anyone with better than 20/400 vision, it was crystal clear as to which one of us would always have to pay an admission charge to get into the Pro Football Hall of Fame.

Put me around a group of jockeys, however, and . . . well . . . you can still spot the outsider, but only because I consume more than a low-carb energy bar and a Diet Coke in any given twenty-four-hour period.

That is the contradicting dichotomy of horse racing. You take the single most powerful performer in any of the world's sports, the Thoroughbred racehorse, and ask the most diminutive member of the sporting community, the jockey, to control its furious strength and speed. It's for that very reason that jockeys, despite their impuissant appearance, deserve to be recognized as skilled and fearless competitors.

And none of these overlooked athletes (pun intended) was better than the great Willie Shoemaker.

Born prematurely and tipping the scale at just over 2 pounds, Shoemaker wasn't expected to live through his first night. According to the stories that came out of that Texas August evening in 1931, Shoemaker was placed in a shoebox in the oven to try and keep him warm. The truth behind the tale hardly matters. It simply serves to underscore the legend of Willie Shoemaker, survivor: a child born with two strikes against him, and a man who bloomed from 2 pounds into one of the giants in all of sports.

At the age of seventeen, and now a robust 4-foot-11 and 96 pounds, Shoemaker rode his first race. A month later, aboard a chestnut filly named Shafter V in a $3,000 claiming race at Golden Gate Fields in California, he rode his first winner, netting himself about $10. On February 3, 1990, at the age of fifty-eight, he rode in his final race. It was two weeks after racing to his final victory, the 8,833rd of his career.

During his forty-two years of riding horses no man rode more mounts or entered the winner's circle with more regularity than Shoemaker. He won eleven Triple Crown races, although the crown itself was never his. He captured ten national money titles while earning more than $123 million in purses. And when ESPN named its top 100 athletes of the twentieth century, Shoemaker came in at No. 57, ahead of Elgin Baylor, Barry Sanders, and Cy Young.

But when it comes to the biggest gaffes on his sport's biggest stage, no one stands taller than Shoemaker.

Having won his first Kentucky Derby aboard Swaps in 1955 (he rode the twelfth-place horse in 1956), Shoemaker entered the 1957 Derby as *the* rising star in racing. And when Gallant

Man's regular jockey, John Choquette, was suspended for rough riding, trainer John Nerud immediately called on Shoe. He accepted the mount, and the history of Churchill Downs would be changed forever.

After a clean break for the field of nine horses and an early lead by Federal Hill, Iron Liege, ridden by Bill Hartack, worked its way to the front. But picking their way up the pack and lurking for a late move were Shoemaker and Gallant Man.

Down the stretch they came, and just as Shoe was able to push Gallant Man into the lead—and apparently into the books as the winner of the eighty-third Run for the Roses—Shoemaker stood up in the saddle to celebrate the win. But what he saw was only the sixteenth pole and not the finish line. And even though Shoe almost immediately recognized the mistake, his momentum had been slowed just enough for Hartack and Iron Liege to recover, and nip him at the wire by the thinnest of noses.

It was an error in the saddle of the worst kind. Because of bad judgment and a premature celebration, Shoemaker had taken away a Kentucky Derby win from Gallant Man and his owner, Ralph Lowe. Rival jockey Eddie Arcaro said of the mistake, "An error like that would have destroyed most men. Only a guy like Willie could have survived it."

Survive it, he did. Shoemaker was suspended for fifteen days by the stewards for the rules violation (standing up in the saddle during a race), and that suspension kept him out of the running of the Preakness fourteen days later. But three weeks after that, again riding astride Gallant Man, Shoemaker and the star-crossed colt decimated the field at Belmont, shattering the track and race records (they would stand until the 1973 Belmont won by Secretariat) and winning the stakes by an incredible eight lengths.

Owner Lowe and trainer Nerud stood by their jockey when the entire world of horse racing was castigating him (not to be confused with the procedure that makes one a gelding) for his Churchill Downs confusion. And that loyalty paid off with

Shoe's winning ride in the Run for the Carnations in Belmont, New York—a loyalty that Shoemaker never forgot.

Shoemaker would have loved for everyone to stop thinking about his mistake in the 1957 Derby. But remembering the grace with which Lowe took that defeat became far more important. In honor of Lowe, Shoemaker endowed a Ralph Lowe trophy, to be awarded annually to the person in racing who best represented sportsmanship—an act that kept alive the memory of Ralph Lowe, the gentleman, as well as, of course, Shoemaker's own greatest embarrassment.

"What a Stupid I Am"
April 14, 1968—The Masters Final Round

People sign their name to things all the time without actually reading the details of what it is they're inking with their legally binding autograph. Ever check in to the hospital? Whatever ailment took you to the hospital originally is quickly forgotten by a newly diagnosed case of carpal tunnel syndrome. Reading all of the information contained on the two dozen trees that were killed to help justify the job of the hospital's overpaid legal department never happens.

And the next time someone reads all of the fine print next to the twenty or so spaces that require initials in order to complete a car-rental transaction will be the first time. If some industrious assistant manager wanted to play a practical joke on the American public, no doubt 99 percent of us would blindly bind our John Hancocks to a page twelve stipulation that returning a car with front-end damage meant the offending party had to get a jumbo-sized, full-color "Avis. We Try Harder" tattoo.

Yet this blasé attitude we have toward ignorantly endorsing legal documents is not without its cautionary tales.

Roberto de Vicenzo was set up for a great 1968. After finishing second or third in the British Open a total of six times, he finally won it in July of 1967, becoming the major's oldest champion. He was playing the best golf of his forty-four-year-old life when the greats of the sport teed up at Augusta for the first major of 1968. When de Vicenzo turned forty-five on Sunday at The Masters, he was within striking distance of capturing the winner's green jacket.

The final round began with Gary Player up by 1 stroke on Bruce Devlin, Don January, Raymond Floyd, Frank Beard, and Bob Goalby. And just 1 stroke behind that fivesome sat de Vicenzo. But before he'd even finished his walk to the 1st green, de Vicenzo had closed the gap between himself and the leader by holing out his 9-iron for an eagle 3.

Birdies fell on the 2nd, 3rd, and 9th holes, and when de Vicenzo made the turn for Augusta's back-nine with a record-tying 31 on the front, he held a 1-stroke lead.

The title was now his to lose.

The birdie onslaught continued, with de Vicenzo picking up strokes against par on the 12th, 15th, and 17th holes. As he strolled to the 18th green, he knew that all he needed was par to finish with a 64 on the day, guaranteeing that the chasing Goalby could only catch him with a birdie on the challenging final hole. But de Vicenzo lipped out his par putt, forcing him to settle for his first and only bogey of the day.

Angered with himself for his final-hole lapse, de Vicenzo went through the motions of signing his scorecard, unable to focus on anything but the door he had opened for Goalby. After quickly scribbling his name, de Vicenzo went to the press room to answer questions from a media ready to pounce. The big story, as far as they were concerned, was his bogey on 18 that would most likely set up an 18-hole playoff the next day.

They couldn't have been more wrong.

Back in the tent where de Vicenzo's signed card still sat

was his playing partner, Tommy Aaron, the man who'd filled it out. And after studying and then signing for his own score, he glanced back over de Vicenzo's. It was wrong. Instead of recording the birdie 3 on the 17th as millions of people witnessed, Aaron had written down a 4 for the hole. And because de Vicenzo had already signed the scorecard, that was the score that would stand.

The news of the mistake spread like wildfire. CBS broadcaster Pat Summerall was told not to mention anything about a possible winner on air. The press room was instructed not to post a score for de Vicenzo, which should have been a 65. And before de Vicenzo ever began speaking to the media in Butler Cabin, the men in green jackets ushered him out.

The rules of golf read:

The competitor is responsible for the correctness of the score recorded for each hole on his scorecard. If he returns a score for any hole lower than actually taken, he is disqualified. If he returns a score for any hole higher than actually taken, the score as returned stands.

No sport is as anal about its rules as golf. And no collection of golfers or golf administrators is as protective of those rules as the men who govern the Augusta National Golf Club. As far as they were concerned, their hands were tied. The final round 66 that de Vicenzo signed for would stand.

Goalby finished with a par-4 on 18, and as he walked off the green he began to think about the playoff to come. Making his way toward the clubhouse, 1955 Masters champion Cary Middlecoff broke the news. "Hey Bob. You won the tournament. Roberto screwed up his card."

His card, his tournament, and his chance to become the oldest Masters champion in history—a record now held by Jack Nicklaus at forty-six years, two months.

When de Vicenzo, always considered one of the nicest men to ever play professional golf, was told of the mistake and what its results would mean, he began to cry.

Inside Butler Cabin for the awarding of the champion's green jacket, de Vicenzo sat defeated and distraught. Goalby was just as upset. His heart broke for his friend, but also for himself. His 66 was the lowest final round ever shot by a Masters champion and his 277 overall was the fourth-lowest in tournament history. But not only would he not be able to celebrate those facts and his declared victory, he would be scorned for it.

In the days and weeks that followed, Goalby received more than five hundred pieces of hate mail, with one author telling him to "burn in hell for eternity." The press said he "won the green jacket with a pencil." And when he was announced on the first tee the following April as the defending Masters champion, several of the fans in attendance actually booed.

Meanwhile, on the other side of the melodrama, de Vicenzo could do no wrong. He estimated that he received more than a million letters and telegrams of support. And directly because of his Augusta flub, de Vicenzo signed a deal with Coca-Cola (he presumably read the contract several times before signing) and made more than $250,000 in endorsements.

Had he won The Masters that year he would have received a winner's check of $20,000.

In an interview the week that he turned eighty-three years old, de Vicenzo called it "the best mistake I ever made." He said that it "opened doors" for him and resulted in more "good things" than almost any of his more than 230 career wins. And the biggest reason for all of that popularity and sympathy? He never blamed anyone but himself.

De Vicenzo could have blamed Tommy Aaron. Or he could have blamed The Masters for being so beholden to the rules. But he never did. Upon learning from Augusta officials about the mistaken scorecard that was sealed case closed by his hastily scrawled signature, Roberto de Vicenzo famously replied, "What a stupid I am."

Crack-up at Carnoustie
July 18, 1999—British Open Final Round

If ever there was a thinking man's sport, it is golf. And if there was ever a sport that consistently rewards smart play over the speculative risk, it is golf.

You no doubt remember the pivotal scene in *Tin Cup*, where in a moment of testosterone inebriation Kevin Costner's character Roy McAvoy empties his bag of balls into the greenside water hazard on the 18th hole, rather than make the smart, easy play and lay up. He ends up holing the 250-yard shot with a fairway wood after dropping it in the drink a half-dozen times and losing the U.S. Open to thickheadedness.

When explaining to his caddie Romeo (poignantly played by Cheech Marin) why he hit the risky shot on 18, even though he didn't need to and even though he'd missed it earlier in the tournament, McAvoy says, "That shot was a defining moment, and when a defining moment comes along, you define the moment . . . or the moment defines you."

It's the kind of sophomoric circular logic that plays well in Hollywood, from a screenwriter trying to sell us on the realism of a driving-range manager in the West Texas town of Salome qualifying for the U.S. Open to win the heart of his rival's girlfriend. But it would never play out like that in the real world. PGA golfers are far too intelligently cautious to let overconfidence cost them a major championship.

At least the non-French ones are.

No Frenchman had won the British Open since Arnaud Massy in 1907. But in 1999 that drought was just 444 yards away from ending. All that separated the relatively unknown Jean Van de Velde—with only one career win to his credit and an Open Championship best finish of thirty-fourth place—from the Claret Jug was Carnoustie's finishing hole known as "home."

Which brings to mind the aphorism *The lights are on but nobody's home*.

Needing no better than a double-bogey 6 on the 18th, a hole he'd birdied in both the second and third rounds, Van de Velde was a lock to win the championship. All he had to do was avoid disaster. And to do that, he simply had to avoid all unnecessary risks. But that pledge for practical play was violated at the tee box.

A tee shot on Carnoustie's 18th is a tricky thing. A long and winding burn (or stream to us Americans) crosses the fairway in two places. But if you opt to club down from the tee, sacrificing distance for accuracy, the burn is taken out of the equation on the tee shot. Van de Velde, however, hit his driver.

Slicing his drive to the right, missing the fairway, and barely missing the burn, Van de Velde was lucky that his ball came to rest on terra firma. But he was *too* lucky. His lie in the rough wasn't that bad, prompting him to go for the green with his second shot instead of making the smart play and lay up. Had the ball been further down in the long rough this ultimately determinative decision would have been made for him by unmowed grass and the physics it presents.

Playing the hole as if he needed a birdie to win, Van de Velde got out his 2-iron. "I only had 185 yards to carry the water, which wasn't very demanding," he said afterward. "The ball was lying so good, but I pushed it a little. I didn't hit a very good shot."

That not-very-good shot hit the grandstand running alongside the right side of the green, bounced back, hit off the top of the rocks on Barry Burn, and landed in the tall grass just short of the burn. Again, he had narrowly avoided the water. But since he had begun the hole with a substantial margin for error, albeit a rapidly closing margin, Van de Velde was still in control of his own destiny.

Until his next shot got tangled in the long grass on his downswing, stripping all of the power from his club and sending the ball directly into the burn. After two narrow misses, Van de Velde was now wet.

This is when the loon came out to play. Thinking that he would just play the ball onto the green from under the water, he took off his shoes and socks, rolled up his pants, and climbed in the burn. But after providing the entire world with the video that would define foolishness in sports for coming generations, Van de Velde reconsidered, opting instead to take a drop.

Now laying four, the frazzled Frenchman was still only an up-and-down away from taking the championship and rendering his three misadventurous shots moot. But instead of getting onto the green and in a position to putt, his 60-yard 5th shot caught the greenside bunker.

"I was really feeling for Jean," said playing partner Craig Parry. "I could see him throwing the tournament away."

Van de Velde's 6th shot finally found the green, and he was able to drain the 6-foot putt for a triple bogey and stay alive in a playoff with Justin Leonard and Paul Lawrie. But after that collapse there was no recovery. He played the first 71 holes of the tournament at 3-over and had his chance to win—a chance only a fool could fumble away. But after a matching 3-over on the tournament's 72nd hole, that chance was gone.

Lawrie, who started that Sunday down by 10 shots, and who never led or co-led once during the regulation 72 holes, won the 4-hole playoff by 3 strokes, giving the Scot his one and only major championship. Van de Velde has never been close since.

He is the name and face of failure under pressure. Repeated bad decisions, coupled with bad play, made the name Jean Van de Velde synonymous with "boneheaded choke."

But even in some golfing circles, his complete name remains

elusive. When Neal Lancaster double-bogeyed the 72nd hole at the 2002 Canadian Open, dropping him into a playoff that he eventually lost, Lancaster said, "I guess I know how Jean-Claude Van Damme, or whatever his name is, felt."

And such is the lack of respect given to golf's forsaken outcast.

Butthead

July 9, 2006—FIFA World Cup Finals, France vs. Italy

Disproportionate overreactions are as European as well-built sports cars, eight-week summer vacations, and emanating bodily odors that go unnecessarily unchecked by society's panoply of perfumed pharmaceuticals.

In 1914 a lone Serbian assassin shot and killed Archduke Francis Ferdinand, the heir to the Austro-Hungarian throne. In response to that one dead royal the Europeans started a war that resulted in another 20 million military and civilian deaths. In Greece the nine-year Trojan War began because three women all reached for the same apple, leading to the kidnapping of Helen. Britain and Iceland have fought three aptly named "Cod Wars" over disputed fishing waters in the North Atlantic. And as depicted with an eye to historical accuracy in the 1975 film *Monty Python and the Holy Grail*, the centuries-old conflict between France and England—fifteen wars, including a pair of Hundred Years' Wars—has been fueled at times by nothing more than catapulting cows and creative French insults about hamsters and elderberries.

In 2006, however, we saw that the French can dish it out, but they most definitely can't take it.

It was the FIFA World Cup Final. Despite how most Americans feel, this is the single biggest sporting event in the world.

In the 2006 World Cup Final, France's Zinedine Zidane loses his cool and lowers his head, drawing the red card that ended his soccer career in shame and cost his nation a chance to win the world's biggest championship. *(© HO/Reuters/Corbis)*

Imagine if the NFL expanded equally across the globe, putting dozens of quality franchises in scores of countries filled with rabid fans of American football. Then imagine if they decided that they would only play the Super Bowl every four years. What would that Super Sunday be like?

And that still falls short of capturing the energy and passion that consumes the world of soccer quadrennially.

In 2006, with an estimated television audience of 715 million (the monthlong tournament had an estimated 26 billion viewers), European rivals France and Italy met for the world title. The Italians, winners of three cups, hadn't quite got over their slim shootout defeat by the French in the 1998 quarterfinals—the year the French went on to claim their only title.

It should also be noted that during that '98 Cup, the French had a near-perfect first round, allowing just one goal in their three Group C victories. The lone blemish on France's first round was the red-card expulsion and two-game suspension of Zinedine Zidane for stomping on Saudi Arabian defender Fuad Amin. Zidane claimed to have been verbally provoked.

Fast-forward now back to 2006, and we're in extra time in the championship game with the score knotted up, 1–1. Suddenly, and apparently out of the blue to the millions of us watching on television, Zidane lowered his head, driving it into the chest of Italian defender Marco Materazzi. Referee Horacio Elizondo didn't see Zidane's aggression, but his assistant did. And after the group of officials conferred on the field, the red card was pulled. In the 110th minute of the World Cup Final, a game Zidane had already declared to be the final of his career, he was disgraced with a match expulsion.

No one scored in extra time, and the game, and championship, had to be decided by penalty kicks. In 1998, when the French edged the Italians in the shootout, 4–3, Zidane easily netted his shot. In the '98 Finals he scored against Brazil. And in the 2006 tournament he had scored in the round of sixteen against Spain and netted penalty kicks in both the semifinals and finals, giving France its lone goal against Italy. Zidane was their star, their clutch performer when the game mattered most. And he would be watching the most important shootout in French soccer history on the locker-room television.

Italy won 5–3, claiming the cup and furthering the disgrace of Zidane.

The condemnation of the star was immediate, as were the questions. What set him off? How could someone so important to the French team lose his temper at such a key moment? What did Materazzi do?

Doing their own detective work, because Zidane wouldn't be specific beyond saying that the Italian used "very hard words," the BBC hired a lip reader to dictate what was said to an Italian translator. And according to her, Materazzi said, "You're the son of a terrorist whore." (Zidane is the son of Algerian immigrants and had been taunted about his heritage throughout his career.)

Materazzi, however, denied saying anything about Zidane's mother, who was in the hospital when all of this played out, saying, "I didn't insult his mother. I lost my mother when I was fifteen and I still get choked up when I talk about it."

Zidane apologized for his actions, calling them inexcusable. But he qualified his "I'm sorrys" by calling Materazzi, the provoker, "the real culprit."

But none of that solved the mystery as to what was said to set Zidane off. Even after FIFA finished its investigation, deciding to fine and suspend both players (since he was retired, Zidane served his three-day sentence doing community service), we still didn't know.

Finally, two months later, Materazzi came clean. While publicly declaring that he would not apologize to Zidane, Materazzi broke his silence on the sequence of events. When the two had tangled in the Italian defensive end, Materazzi grabbed Zidane's jersey, prompting the Frenchman to bark sarcastically, "If you really want my shirt you can have it later."

Materazzi then, according to his own account, replied, "I prefer the whore that is your sister."

And with that insult the Holy Grail of soccer trophies was lost for the French, and the career of Zinedine Zidane, a three-time FIFA World Player of the Year and the winner of the 2006 World Cup Golden Ball (the MVP of the World Cup), was over.

Ice Capades
January 6, 1994—U.S. Figure Skating Championships

As one famous deep-thinking American philosopher said, gleaning considerable wisdom from his experiences as a college football All-American, soldier in Vietnam, and world-touring professional Ping-Pong player, "Stupid is as stupid does."

Don't think for one minute that it's a coincidence that Forrest Gump's familiar phrase entered the consciousness of American moviegoers when his self-titled autobiographical film was released just six days after the U.S. Figure Skating Association stripped Tonya Harding of her 1994 national championship and banned her from the sport for life.

Forrest, self-admittedly "not a smart man," had a particular knack for spotting stupid. When it comes to Tonya Harding and the collection of simpleminded stooges who plotted and perpetrated the attack on Harding's skating rival, Nancy Kerrigan, the extreme low end of the Wechsler Adult Intelligence Scale—the scale used to classify mental acumen, or lack thereof—had to be rewritten.

Using the scientific measurements of the WAIS, Harding, ex-husband Jeff Gillooly, Harding bodyguard Shawn Eckhardt, assailant Shane Stant, and getaway driver Derrick Smith are technically classified as *barely functional half-witted boobs.*

Harding's slide downhill, from the skating sensation who captured the 1991 U.S. Figure Skating Championship and the first American woman to land a triple axel in the World Figure Skating Championships later that year, began long before she green-lighted the whacking of Kerrigan's knee before the '94 national championships in Detroit.

Harding, a high school dropout when she was a sophomore, was most certainly not cut from the same cloth as previous U.S. figure-skating champions (think Peggy Fleming, Dorothy Hamill, and Debi Thomas). Harding was an asthmatic but also a smoker. She struggled with her training, and her weight was inconsistent. She was often late to competitions, arriving so late to the 1992 Winter Olympics that while she was performing in the Games, the most important competition of her life, she was still dealing with jet lag from the flight to France.

In 1993 the wheels really began to come off . . . literally. At Skate America that year Harding famously stopped skating in the middle of her performance, complaining that a blade on her skate had become loose. At the '93 U.S. Figure Skating Championships she asked the referee if she could restart her short program because the back of her dress had become unhooked. Harding had been given a waiver of qualification for those championships after an anonymous bomb threat was phoned in against her prior to the Pacific Coast Sectional.

The FBI later revealed that there was evidence that Harding allegedly participated in placing the threat herself.

So the leap to go from bomb-threat maker to hired-hit conspirator against her stiffest competition at the 1994 U.S. national championships was nothing more than a single toe loop for this Portland, Oregon, queen of jumps. After all, no one was going to be injured permanently. Or you could convince yourself of that fiction, if in the haze of your own ambition you were blinded to the intended permanent damage that the attack was to do to Nancy Kerrigan's Olympic dreams. But for this pack of fools, that was a line of morality that never existed.

The attack—a clubbing to Kerrigan's right knee that reportedly cost the conspirators $6,000—was carried out on January 6, just after she left a practice session the day before the national championships. And it achieved the desired effect. Kerrigan was knocked out of the competition and Harding went on to win it, securing her spot on the U.S. Olympic team.

But in less than a week the plot, in all its glorious twists and absurdities, fell apart like Harding's dilapidated rural Oregon trailer home.

Just one day after Harding's championship, Kerrigan was voted onto the Olympic team by the U.S. Figure Skating Association. They used a seldom-used rule that allowed them to place skaters on the team who didn't compete in the Olympic trials. Then, just days later, and after the weapon used against Kerrigan was found, media reports began to surface that the FBI was investigating Gillooly and Eckhardt for hatching the plot. A tape recording had surfaced of the two criminal masterminds discussing the planned assault.

Arrests of the pair followed, with it taking almost no time for these two licentious weasels to start implicating Harding. She, of course, initially denied any knowledge of the attack, slowly amending that to an admission of knowing about the plot, but only after the fact. But when Gillooly pleaded guilty to racketeering in connection with the assault and agreed to testify against Harding for being an active participant in the preplot planning, things truly blew up for Harding and the United States Olympic Committee.

The USOC immediately began action to remove Harding from the Olympic team. But after Harding filed a $20 million lawsuit and a court-ordered block on the hearing that could get her booted from the team (and lawyers wonder why we hate them), the USOC was forced to relent, lest the protracted legal battle drag the entire Olympics through Harding's disgusting mud.

Of course, as was vividly played out in the absurd display of Harding and Kerrigan practicing together on the ice in Lillehammer, Norway, the legal wranglings brought on by this pullulating pariah couldn't have been half as putrid as her presence turned out to be. Or as distracting as the four-hundred-member-strong throng of media that reported on the pair's every Norwegian step.

As evidence of an omnipotent and just deity, Kerrigan won the Olympic silver medal and Harding finished an embarrassing eighth, while setting a world record in the race to become skating's persona non grata. But Harding's fall was still in its early stages.

Gillooly's interview with the FBI detailed Harding's role in the plot, alleging that she made the final call to go through with the attack, telling him, "Okay, let's do it." And he claimed that it was Harding who called a magazine writer to find out where Kerrigan practiced in Massachusetts, and then she called the rink to find out when. Gillooly also told the FBI that when the plot moved from Boston to Detroit, Harding complained to him that no one appeared able "to do this thing for me."

Destined to be damned, Harding quickly pleaded guilty to hindering the investigation, which saved her from any jail time and allowed her to officially maintain the position that she hadn't participated in the planning—a claim that is not only laughable, but also refuted by Gillooly and Eckhardt, who told authorities Harding said to Gillooly, "Stop screwing around with this and get it done."

Gillooly was sentenced to two years in prison, of which he spent six months behind bars. Eckhardt spent a year in prison while Stant, the attacker, served fourteen months of his eighteen-month sentence. The same sentence was handed down to Stant's getaway driver, Derrick Smith.

For Harding, the sentence, however, has been life: a life of living as a late-night punch line and holding a place in society just below that of carnival freak.

There was the release of her homemade porno. Uh . . . no thanks. There were her very public run-ins with alcohol, one of which landed her in jail for assaulting her then-boyfriend with a hubcap, presumably from the pickup truck she had previously driven into a ditch or the aforementioned trailer in which she was making a home. In my personal favorite post-Olympic Harding moment, she once claimed that a professional golfer in Oregon had started stalking her. On second thought, that also may need to be filed under "run-ins with alcohol."

And then there was her "check your dignity at the door" appearance on Fox TV's *Celebrity Boxing*, where she beat Paula "I've Got a Target on My Face the Size of Bill Clinton's . . . Presidential Library" Jones. That foolishly led her to believe that a professional boxing career was in her future—a future that mercifully lasted just six ridiculously bad bouts but did provide us with one final laugh and proof that old habits die hard. Harding canceled a scheduled bout in March of 2004 (see "too scared to fight") because of an alleged death threat she received.

As if at this point anyone really cares enough to try and do her harm. The only criminals lame enough to waste their time with her would be the same collaborating clowns she was in cahoots with back in 1994. Assuming that their felonious skills haven't sharpened significantly over the years, I think she's safe.

Goodyear, Bad Day
May 28, 1995—Indianapolis 500

It's called "the Greatest Spectacle in Racing." Winning the Indianapolis 500 and taking the traditional swig of milk in the winner's circle is said to be a racer's greatest thrill. It also happens to be a thrill that Scott Goodyear knows nothing about, through plenty of his own fault.

At the Brickyard, 1995 was a transitional year. The newly formed Indy Racing League and its split with CART dominated the prerace news, with both bodies threatening to stage competing seasons the following year, driving open-wheeled racing even further into the growing shadow of NASCAR. The '95 race was going to be run without two of its biggest names driving for its most prestigious team. Roger Penske drivers Emerson Fittipaldi, a two-time champion at Indy, and Al Unser Jr., the race's defending champion, both failed to qualify after a rules change shifted the edge away from Penske's special pushrod engine.

Change was sweeping across the Indiana plain. With the old guard relegated to spectator status, no one quite knew what to expect from the seventy-ninth running of America's oldest automobile race. Certainly no one could have predicted the idiocracy that was to come.

When it was over and the roaring engines had finally quieted across Speedway, Indiana, Canadian Jacques Villeneuve was the last racer standing—the youngest driver to win the race since 1952. But the series of events that carried him to the checkered flag were like none other seen in the history of the race.

On lap 190, with just 25 miles to go, and with what was shaping up to be an incredible final stretch duel between Villeneuve and Goodyear, Goodyear passed the one car you never want to. Coming out of a caution on the fourth turn, Goodyear sped past the pace car before it had extinguished its yellow caution lights and entered the pit road—a serious racing no-no.

Track officials immediately spotted the infraction and black-flagged Goodyear to the pits for a penalty—a penalty that would essentially eliminate him from race contention. So Goodyear, believing that he did nothing wrong, ignored it. He stayed on the track instead of heading for the pits. And when the official scorers removed him from the leaderboard on lap 195, disqualifying him from the race, Goodyear drove on.

The first man to cross the finish line after completing 500 miles was Scott Goodyear. But with his DQ on the 195th lap, officially he ranked only 14th in the field. Villeneuve was the winner.

Stubborn is one thing. Insistence in the heat of the competitive moment is another. But divorcing yourself from reality and acting like an eight-year-old Little Leaguer who refuses to leave second base even though he was clearly tagged out is something entirely different. Goodyear actually had the audacity to say that he was "in disbelief" when track officials didn't award him the trophy after he crossed the finish line, boldly, and quite stupidly, proclaiming, "Everyone throughout the world knows who won this race."

We sure do, Scott. Jacques Villeneuve.

Goodyear defended his passing of the pace car by claiming that he was simply trying to avoid a rear-end collision. He alleged that at 80 mph—Goodyear was traveling at 150 mph when the race was restarted—the pace car was traveling too slowly, a complaint he shared with several other drivers throughout the race. In fact, a similar penalty had been handed to another driver earlier in the race for a pace car infraction.

That driver? Jacques Villeneuve.

That's right. The man who eventually won the race was forced to sit out two laps at the 100-mile mark for failing to let pace driver Don Bailey and his Corvette get in front of him when the yellow caution flag came out. Villeneuve claimed at the time that he didn't realize he was leading, which would have made his efforts to stay ahead of the pace car, and staying on the lead lap, legal. But even with that discrepancy, Villeneuve served his punishment. He didn't blame or bemoan, he just drove, determinedly bringing himself from five miles down to get back into the lead by the time the checkered flag flew.

And because of that penalty and the race he had to run, Villeneuve rejected any mention about his win being tainted.

"I expected him to be penalized," he said of Goodyear. "You can't overtake the pace car. If they penalize us earlier, they were going to penalize him. Just because it's the Indy 500 and you've been racing for two hours, you can't ignore the rules."

The president of the USAC, the body in charge of the race, was quick to defend Bailey's driving. And Tom Binford, the chief steward, said, "It's the pace car driver's responsibility to mosey through that turn at a speed that is responsible."

Speaking of responsible, the day following the race Steve

Horne, Goodyear's boss, admitted that after watching replays of the restart that an obvious infraction did in fact occur. The responsibility for the given penalty, and therefore the lost opportunity to win the Indianapolis 500, was Goodyear's.

In 1992 Goodyear finished just 0.043 seconds behind the winner, Al Unser Jr. In 1997 he again finished second, losing to Arie Luyendyk on a controversial final-lap restart. But neither of those near misses weighed as heavily on Goodyear as the debacle of '95. For that loss, there was no one to blame but himself.

Tastes Like Champion
June 28, 1997—Mike Tyson vs. Evander Holyfield

One of the many great things about being a human—as opposed to, say, a squirrel or hedgehog—is that we are at the top of the food chain. Other than the occasional great white shark scuba snack or lost hiker who fails to practice good bear safety, none of us are at risk of becoming a savory meal. Even culturally accepted cannibalism, as opposed to what the Donner Party practiced as a means of survival, is largely a thing of the past. Assuming that you don't run into the likes of Jeffrey Dahmer or find yourself at odds with a Congolese witch doctor who thinks your pureed appendages will provide his warrior pygmy tribe the fountain of youth, you probably won't get eaten.

In sports, that place on top of the food chain is even more secure. Other than the marooned Uruguayan rugby team featured in the book and film *Alive*, the world of sports has been relatively cannibal free. However, we can forgive the sixteen survivors of the 1972 plane crash in the Andes. They were simply trying to live. But with today's ready access to high-protein energy bars it's hard to imagine any reasonable justification for Mike Tyson's bite out of Evander Holyfield.

Of course, Tyson's lived an entire life without having to keep a standard.

Long before the most famous midbout carbo loading in boxing history took place in Las Vegas in 1997, the human freak show that is Mike Tyson was heading for a disastrous end. Let's be honest. While the act of biting Holyfield's ear was shocking, who truly was surprised by Tyson's morph into man-eater? The boxing world and all of Tyson's many apologists reaped what they sowed.

We all knew what he was, even when the stupidest university president in the history of higher education invited Tyson to Central State University in Ohio to receive an honorary doctorate. While accepting the degree Tyson told the commencement crowd, which included donors, dignitaries, and more than a few grandparents of graduating seniors, "I don't know what kind of doctor I am, but watching all of these beautiful sisters here, I'm debating if I should be a gynecologist." Classy.

The organizers of the Miss Black America pageant knew what they were getting when they invited Tyson to their pageant in 1991. By this time Tyson, who was quoted in a biography saying that the best punch he ever threw was one that hit ex-wife Robin Givens ("She flew backward, hitting every [expletive] wall in the apartment"), was known to be opprobrious to women. And no one can legitimately claim to be surprised that he was convicted of raping pageant contestant Desiree Washington. That was who he was.

But he never had to answer for his actions or pay for them in certain circles in the court of public opinion. Three months after Tyson was released from an Indiana prison, a welcome home party was planned for him in New York. The welcome, which acted as if Tyson was returning to America after serving the underprivileged abroad instead of serving three years in state prison for rape, boasted a committee of community leaders that featured Representative Charles Rangel and Rev. Al Sharpton.

Never has a man who could do no wrong done so much of it.

After prison Tyson regained the heavyweight titles of the WBC and WBA with wins over Frank Bruno and Bruce Seldon—only to lose them both in November 1996, when he lost to underdog Evander Holyfield and proved that he was nowhere close to being the feared fighter that he'd been prior to incarceration. But Tyson was still a draw, even with fading skills, and with the highest-paid purses in boxing history ($30 million for Tyson and $35 million for Holyfield), the rematch at the MGM Grand was set for June 28 of the following year.

It didn't take long for the much-hyped bout to take a sharp turn to the bizarre. After sustaining a cut over his eye in the second round because of an incidental butt of heads, Tyson came out for the third round without his mouthpiece. Referee Mills Lane sent Tyson back to his corner to get his mouthpiece, and the round commenced.

The two exchanged combinations, with Tyson being a somewhat careless aggressor throughout the round. And then suddenly, with about forty seconds to go before the bell, and before what was actually playing out between the two fighters registered with any of the ringside observers, Holyfield pushed his way out of a clinch and began hopping up and down in pain while holding his ear.

No one really knew what had happened until the slow-mo replay. The video showed in precise detail that while the two men were in a clinch, Tyson spit out his mouthpiece, rolled his head above Holyfield's shoulder, and took a very deliberate bite out of Holyfield's right ear. It was too crazy for words.

And because that wasn't quite enough to drop Tyson to the bottom of the genetic chain of human evolution, when the fight resumed after a several-minute delay, Tyson immediately did it again—this time getting Holyfield's left ear.

The round ended without any further damage to the facial features of the champion Holyfield. But once Lane realized that a second bite had taken place, he stopped the fight before the fourth round began.

With word of Lane's decision, Tyson's corner blew up in anger (presumably because Tyson had an appetite that was yet to be satisfied), prompting him to go after both Holyfield and Holyfield's trainer, swinging at anyone and everyone who tried to get in his way, including a police officer. That boiling anger and outrage eventually spilled out of the ring and into the crowd, with three people injured in the following melee that briefly included Tyson climbing over a railing to pick a fight with a fan who'd showered him with water.

The arena riot was briefly quieted when ring announcer Jimmy Lennon Jr. read the unprecedented decision: "Referee Mills Lane has disqualified Mike Tyson for biting Evander Holyfield on both of his ears."

It still reads as freakishly outlandish all these years later. But really, it was who he was.

That June night in Las Vegas the book was essentially closed on the sideshow that was Mike Tyson. After serving a year suspension for the multiple ear chomps, Tyson fought and beat Francois Botha. But a month after that, he was back in prison for assaulting a pair of motorists following a traffic accident.

When Tyson was released from his second stint behind bars, he resumed his professional boxing career, sort of. He fought a series of "tomato cans" and twice had fights end with a "no contest" because of controversies involving the former champ—imagine that.

Tyson was able to finagle his way into a fight with Lennox Lewis in 2002, briefly considering more cannibalism ("I want your heart, I want to eat your children") and making a mockery of anyone who thinks Tyson is no longer the woman-hating misogynist that he was with Robin Givens and Desiree Washington. When a female reporter asked Tyson a question as he was preparing to face Lewis, Tyson replied, "I normally don't do interviews with women unless I fornicate with them. So you shouldn't talk anymore . . . unless you want to, you know."

At the time Tyson was married to a pediatrician.

Tyson lost to Lewis, badly, and finally left the world of boxing for good after getting knocked out by Danny Williams and quitting in the middle of his fight with Kevin McBride.

In 1987 Tyson became the first heavyweight to own the three major championship belts—WBA, WBC, and IBF—at the same time. But when the name Mike Tyson is spoken, who remembers that? Or even finds it relevant? Not me.

Lost in the Vault
June 27, 1992—U.S. Olympic Trials

Any advertising wonk worth his weight in gross rating points is familiar with Leo Burnett. The legendary advertising executive who was responsible for the Jolly Green Giant, Toucan Sam, the Pillsbury Doughboy, and Tony the Tiger transformed the industry in the 1930s by replacing its practice of creating lengthy arguments for a product's worthiness with wrapping a product around an image. Perhaps the most enduring of Burnett's creations, and one of the most famous figures in all of advertising, was the Marlboro Man. He was the unabashedly masculine man's man, living carefree in the open West, with nothing but the setting sun and the occasional cattle drive to guide his days. He was the man all other men wished they were.

The no-doubt very-well-educated advertising people working for Reebok in 1992 understood the power of a single, desirable, wished-for image. They didn't try to sell us the spring-back ratio of the Reebok sole or the in-use weight/volume vs. converted kinetic energy formula that made Reebok superior to the other athletic shoes on the market. They told us to buy Reebok

Decathlete Dan O'Brien misses his second attempt at the pole vault at the 1992 U.S. Olympic Trials, setting up the third and final, and fateful, miss that knocked him off the U.S. Olympic team. *(Thom Scott/AFP/Getty Images)*

because the two most recognizable men competing that summer for the title of World's Greatest Athlete wore the shoe: Dan O'Brien and Dave Johnson.

The "Dan and Dave" campaign cost Reebok millions of dollars. But it was as close to a can't lose as there was in the industry. They were both good-looking, clean-cut, and engaging men, gifted with an athleticism that the rest of us dare not dream of. And they would be going head-to-head in Barcelona for the Olympic gold medal in the decathlon—the sport that turned Bruce Jenner into a product-promoting giant.

If you had a working television in the first half of 1992 you knew and liked "Dan and Dave," and you most likely knew that Reebok was responsible for putting them on your TV every twenty minutes. You were also circling August 5 and 6 on your calendar: the dates of the most anticipated two-day competition in the history of decathlon.

Men's basketball wasn't the only sport that would be boasting a Dream Team at the '92 Games. The U.S. decathlon team was every bit as celebrated. Right up until the very moment that world-record holder Dan O'Brien failed to qualify at the U.S. Olympic Trials.

For those of you unfamiliar with the decathlon and how it's scored, it's a series of ten track-and-field events held over the course of two days. Since each of the events uses different measures of success (time, distance, height), the athletes are given a point score based on how well they do in that particular event. For example, if the competitor completes the 100-meter dash in eleven seconds flat (the first of the ten events), he would be awarded 861 points, regardless of where he ranked among the rest of the field.

O'Brien, as the defending world champion, would be the unchallenged gold-medal favorite in Barcelona, with perhaps his stiffest competition expected to come from Goodwill Games champion Dave Johnson, the senior member of the U.S. team. With all eyes on that Barcelona showdown, the U.S. trials held in New Orleans were almost a forgotten afterthought. Even though the two most celebrated decathletes in the world were doing battle at Tad Gormley Stadium, only 16,717 fans bought tickets. The real contest wouldn't come for another six weeks.

Through seven events everything was going according to plan. O'Brien was leading and on pace for a new world record, while Johnson was comfortably in second place and with his best event, the javelin, still to come. Up next, the pole vault.

In warm-ups O'Brien was easily clearing 16 feet 1 inch in

the vault. So he passed on the opening heights of 14'5½", 14'9", 15'1", and 15'5", electing to start his quest for the world record at 15'9". But in his first attempt, he missed, knocking down the crossbar.

Bruce Jenner, a former world-record holder and gold-medal champion at the 1976 Montreal Olympics, described how a first miss on your opening height is a recipe for disaster.

"You miss the first, and you start to panic," he said. "You miss the second, and you go numb. On the third attempt you have no chance."

Panicking, O'Brien again hit the crossbar on his second attempt. And then, numb, he didn't even make it that high on his third attempt. He had missed. He was done. Instead of the expected 900 or more points for O'Brien on the pole vault, he got a zero, ending his dreams of gold in Barcelona. If he was going to Spain, he'd now have to buy his own ticket.

Said a stunned O'Brien, "I wanted to turn to someone and say, 'Do something.'"

Johnson, powerless to help his friend and fellow competitor, admitted to nearly crying. "I was pretty upset. We're a team. I walked to him, said I was sorry, and gave him a hug."

Within ten minutes of O'Brien's final pole-vault miss, Reebok instructed NBC to pull all of the "Dan and Dave" commercials for the remainder of the meet's telecast and replace them with Reebok ads featuring Roger Clemens and Rocket Ismail. Such is the fickle nature of the here today, gone tomorrow (literally) world of a celebrity spokesperson.

Life did go on for Dan O'Brien. The Reebok ads continued, now themed with a resolute Dan cheerleading for Dave in Barcelona—where he ended up with a bronze medal. A month after the '92 Olympics O'Brien set a world record with 8,891 points. And in 1996 he won an Olympic gold medal with 8,824 points.

In June of that year O'Brien made the U.S. Olympic team on

the strength of a pole vault of 17 feet ¾ inch. In 1992 he would have made the team with a vault of only 9 feet 2¼ inches.

And then maybe he would have been a double gold medalist in the Olympics' most illustrious event.

Missing in Munich
Munich Olympics 1972—Men's 5,000-Meter Finals

It's the nightmare of any athlete with an early call time: the failing alarm clock causes you to miss the start of your event, and you miss the moment you've been training for all your life.

It happened to a New York City Marathon runner in 1995.

His name was Jean-Paul Jean-Paul. After doubts arose about the woman charged with making sure that he would be awake in time for the race, and after the hotel that became plan B turned out to have a less-than-trustworthy desk clerk responsible for wake-up calls, Jean-Paul had the misfortune of spending race eve in an apartment building that suffered a freak power outage. With his alarm clock powered off, he overslept, only making it to the marathon after a frantic dash to the starting line threw off his prerace preparation, ultimately costing him a chance at victory.

Of course, usually world-class athletes getting ready for the event of their lives don't have to hurdle their way past an overly anal Jerry Seinfeld, an unreliable Elaine Benes, or the power-taxing heat pump of Cosmo Kramer's hot tub. It's comedy, not reality. An athlete of that caliber on such an important day would have backups for their backup fail-safes. If, say, Olympic gold is at stake, you make no mistakes and leave absolutely nothing to chance.

In 1972 that should have been the mind-set for Ethiopian distance runner Miruts Yifter. He should have been dotting all of his Is and crossing all Ts—especially after an embarrassing entry onto the international scene a year earlier during a meet in North Carolina. Because Yifter was unfamiliar with Arabic numbers, he miscalculated the lap count in the 5,000 meters, beginning his final kick much too soon and burning himself out down the stretch, allowing American Steve Prefontaine to easily take the win.

You would think that with that blunder on his résumé Yifter and his coaches would have been extra careful. Well, you would think wrong.

Having already taken the bronze medal in the 10,000 meters, Yifter's weaker event, he was considered a cinch to win gold in the 5,000. Yifter's humiliation in North Carolina would soon be nothing but an afterthought after the glory that he was about to achieve for himself and Ethiopia at the Olympic Stadium in Munich. It was a sports-clichéd case of just having to show up.

Unfortunately, he didn't.

The 5,000 meter finals began, and Miruts Yifter was a no-show. What exactly happened to him that day still remains a mystery. Stories range from him getting lost in the stadium's tunnels to having an impromptu restroom break that went longer than originally expected. Yifter's own, unconfirmed, explanation places the blame on his coaches. Yifter claims, "My coaches took me to the mixed zone to warm up, and left me there. But then, they arrived late, and by the time they took me to the race marshals the race had already begun."

Maybe that happened. But maybe I don't wait on my coaches if they're running late. Maybe I take it upon myself to get my gold-medal-favorite butt to the starting line on time. But maybe that's just me.

Instead of Yifter's expected return home as a conquering Olympic hero, many Ethiopian officials tagged him a traitor who had "deliberately" missed the 5,000 finals. And according to them, the public and private shame that he was enduring was not punishment enough. So they threw him in prison for three months, releasing him just in time for the All-Africa Games of 1973, where he finally won gold.

But Olympic gold was an entirely different matter. It was also a dream that couldn't be realized until 1976. But instead of heading to Montreal as the likely favorite to win redemption, Yifter spent those Olympics stuck in Ethiopia. New Zealand's All Blacks rugby team had toured South Africa earlier in the year. Because the IOC didn't then ban New Zealand from the 1976 Games, twenty-eight African nations, including Ethiopia, boycotted. Yifter's dream was once again on hold for another four years.

Say what you will about this quirky and mysterious man who made one of the biggest blunders in Olympic history. A man who, when asked about his age on the eve of the 1980 Olympics, replied, "Men may steal my chickens; men may steal my sheep. But no man may steal my age." A man who may have been more than a little nutty. But he was also a man driven like few others. Eight years after he'd failed to show for certain Olympic gold in Munich, and four years after the 1976 Olympics were taken away because of politics, he finally climbed to the top of the medal stand in Moscow, twice, winning gold in both the 10,000 and 5,000 meters.

Very few men are talented enough to carry the competing titles of double Olympic champion and formerly jailed Olympic goat.

MEDIA

There is a famous story involving Hall of Fame pitcher Dizzy Dean after he'd turned broadcaster in the 1950s. Dean was calling a game on television one Saturday afternoon when the camera kept panning to a young couple making out in the stands. As the story goes, Dean commented on air to broadcast partner Pee Wee Reese, "Look at that, Pee Wee. He's kissing her on the strikes, and she's kissing him on the balls."

Sadly, the story's truth is hard to confirm. Even Snopes.com has taken up the cause of proving or disproving the tale of Dean's double entendre but to no avail. It certainly sounds like something the colorful, and often off-color, Dean would say. And as a story over the decades it definitely has legs. It has been told and retold hundreds of times, and by now it has made its way into the archives of numerous credible sources.

Anyone who has watched any amount of sports television knows that broadcasters say all kinds of regrettable things. When I was a writer for Fox Sports I witnessed one of our reporters, who shall remain nameless to protect the not so innocent, ask one of the Lakers live during coverage of the NBA Finals what music got him fired up before game time. The Laker replied, "Tupac."

To which our intrepid reporter said, "Perhaps you can convince Tupac to perform at the victory parade if you guys win."

The year was 2000. Tupac Shakur was shot to death in 1996.

But compared to many of the gaffes and lapses in journalistic judgment that have plagued the men and women who bring us the images and descriptions of our favorite sporting events, suggesting that a dead member of the Hip-Hop Museum and Hall of Fame might perform one of his nineteen top-10 *Billboard* hits at a championship victory parade in downtown Los Angeles ranks pretty low. And once you read about the media mistakes that rank high enough to warrant a place in this book of blunders, you'll clearly see why.

The Heidi Game
November 17, 1968—Jets vs. Raiders

Chances are that sometime between the ages of ten and fourteen you became familiar with the charming nineteenth-century Swiss girl named Heidi. Either by way of a school assignment, reading the book on your own, or having your sister describe her to you in excruciating detail, you learned all about this delightful young orphan who warmed the heart of her cantankerous and secluded grandfather. Who can forget the welling of tears when, after years away in Frankfurt, Heidi returned to Switzerland, prompting her grandfather to come down the mountain and to the village for the first time in years to greet her. Oh, how they laughed.

I know what you're thinking. If ever there was a plot fit for a group of guys hopped up on beer and football-induced testosterone, this is it. Nothing goes with Sunday football quite like

While the Raiders' Preston Ridlehuber (37) picked up the Jets' fumbled kickoff and scored the touchdown that sealed a critical November victory for Oakland over New York (can you guess which picture?), football fans watching on NBC were instead treated to the made-for-TV movie *Heidi*. "Treated" is my word, not theirs. *(© Bettmann/Corbis)*

nine-year-old Swiss Alp goatherds teaching each other to read and write. In fact, if I was a television executive at NBC, I'd figure out a way to combine the two things, and pronto.

Actually, my brilliant entertainment idea has already been done. Through a series of bad pregame decisions and late-game communication breakdowns, the rare—and never since repeated—doubleheader of shortened professional football and beloved children's tale was broadcast across the nation in 1968.

Forty years ago football rarely, if ever, took more than three hours to complete. So with a new made-for-TV version of *Heidi* set to air that November Sunday night on NBC at 7:00 p.m. eastern, no one thought the Jets-Raiders game beginning at 4:00 p.m. eastern (1:00 p.m. kickoff in Oakland) would be a problem. Just in case the game did bleed past seven o'clock, to avoid any confusion a decision on what to do had already been made: roll *Heidi*. There were prime-time sponsors to think about.

With sixty-five seconds remaining in the fourth quarter, the Jets took a 32–29 lead on Jim Turner's fourth field goal of the game. New York then kicked off, and the Raiders returned it to their own 23-yard line to set up a last-minute drive to try and tie or win the game. And then NBC went to commercial.

If you were in the eastern or central time zones, that's the last you saw of the game.

When Raiders quarterback Daryle Lamonica hit Charlie Smith up the field, and a face-mask penalty moved the ball to the Jets' 43, NBC viewers saw actress Jennifer Edwards frolicking through a hillside meadow. On the very next play, when Lamonica and Smith hooked up for a lead-taking touchdown pass, NBC viewers saw Aunt Dete, Heidi's caretaker until the age of six, leaving Heidi with her Alm-Öhi (Alp-grandfather, as he was known). And when the Jets fumbled the following kickoff by Oakland and the Raiders recovered and carried the ball into the end zone for their second touchdown in nine seconds, NBC viewers were treated to Heidi's initial meeting with her soon-to-be new best friend, Peter the goatherd. Viewers were finally informed of the final score via a crawl along the bottom of their television screens, just as Heidi's paralytic cousin Clara was taking her first timid steps.

A lot of things were working against NBC that day. For one, there were 19 penalties called in the game, slowing its pace to a crawl and causing the conflict in programming. And even though earlier executives had told NBC broadcast operations supervisor Dick Cline to make sure he started *Heidi* on time, those same executives changed their minds late in the game. But because there were so many football fans calling NBC to request that the network stick with the game and delay the movie, the execs couldn't get through the switchboard.

"I waited and I waited and I heard nothing," said Cline. "We came up on that magic hour and I thought, 'Well, I haven't been given any counter order so I've got to do what we agreed to do.'"

The flood of phone calls that then poured in after the switch to *Heidi* completely blew the switchboard.

In a statement released ninety minutes later NBC president Julius Goodman tried to defuse the anger by calling the decision "a forgivable error committed by humans who were concerned about children expecting to see *Heidi*. I missed the game as much as anyone else."

Predictably the anger did not subside. Fans spent the rest of the night complaining to NBC affiliates, radio stations, newspapers, and even the New York Police Department. The next morning the story of the game and NBC's programming decision made the front page of the *New York Times*.

There was certainly no sympathy coming NBC's way from its rival networks. On *CBS Evening News with Walter Cronkite*, Harry Reasoner reported the outcome of the game: "Heidi married the goat-herder." And Monday on *ABC Evening News* anchor Frank Reynolds read aloud from Johanna Spyri's novel while sportscaster Howard Cosell repeatedly interrupted him with highlights and commentary from the game's final minute.

The one saving grace for NBC in all of this was that the incident completely changed the way we watch football on Sundays.

There is now language in every NFL television contract that stipulates that the games of visiting teams will always be shown to their home markets in their entirety. And football fans across the country can now recite this CBS disclaimer, verbatim: "Immediately following the conclusion of our game, *60 Minutes* will be seen in its entirety, except on the West Coast."

And for that we can thank a fictitious Swiss girl named Heidi.

It's All Greek to Me
January 15, 1988—Washington, D.C.

When given the choice, I think we all would prefer to be judged by our actions and not our words. We seem to say really dumb things far more often than we do them. And when you spend a great deal of your time speaking into a microphone that will record those words for all eternity, those dumb things can take on a life of their own.

Former vice president Dan Quayle has a law degree from Indiana University. But he will forever be the guy who spelled potato "p-o-t-a-t-o-e." When Barack Obama was running against Hillary Clinton in the 2008 Democratic primary, the Harvard- and Columbia-educated candidate—then in Oregon—said, "Over the last fifteen months we've traveled to every corner of the United States. I've now been in fifty-seven states; now one left to go." Brooke Shields, who has a French-literature degree from Princeton University, said, upon becoming a spokesperson for a federal anti-smoking campaign, "Smoking kills. And once you've been killed, you've lost a very important part of your life."

Obviously Barack Obama did not think, back in May 2008, that our country has 58 states. Of course Brooke Shields understands that being killed takes your whole life and not just an "important part" of it. And does anyone really think that Dan Quayle doesn't know how to spell potato? Okay, he's a bad example. But you get the idea.

People say dumb things all of the time. We shouldn't automatically assume that their words define them. For example, we shouldn't automatically assume that Jimmy "the Greek" Snyder was a racist, just because of what he said that got him fired by CBS Sports.

You no doubt remember the man. For twelve years he was an analyst and prognosticator on the CBS pregame show *The NFL Today*. As a guy who made it to national sports television by way of working as an oddsmaker in Las Vegas, he was often criticized for taking gambling mainstream—an image that was only reinforced by a cameo in the 1981 film *The Cannonball Run*, in which Snyder laid 50-to-1 odds on the team of Dean Martin and Sammy Davis Jr. winning the coast-to-coast car race.

He was also very rightly skewered for the things he said on January 15, 1988—Martin Luther King Jr.'s birthday, no less.

During lunch at Duke Zeibert's restaurant in D.C., Ed Hotaling of NBC affiliate WRC asked Snyder to comment on the progress of black athletes in American sports, since it was the anniversary of King's birthday. Snyder replied:

> *The black is a better athlete to begin with because he's been bred to be that way—because of his high thighs and big thighs that goes up into his back, and they can jump higher and run faster because of their bigger thighs. This goes all the way back to the Civil War when during slave trading, the owner—the slave owner would breed his big black to his big woman so that he could have a big black kid.*

Clearly not a sociologist or historian, Snyder went on to say:

> *If blacks take over coaching the way everyone wants them to there won't be anything left for the white people. I mean, all*

the players are black. The only thing the whites control is the coaching.

And just in case he hadn't fully insulted everyone, Snyder finished with:

Whites are lazy. There's ten players on a basketball court. If you find two whites you're lucky. Four out of five, or nine out of ten are black. Now that's because they practice and play, and practice and play. They're not lazy like the white athlete is.

That, as they say, was all she wrote. The comments aired on *CBS Evening News with Dan Rather* that night, and by the next day Snyder was looking for work. CBS Sports quickly cut all ties with Snyder and said in a statement, "In no way do these comments reflect the view of CBS Sports."

Snyder issued an apology the same day his statements were broadcast across the country, saying, "I'm truly sorry for my remarks earlier today and I offer a full, heartfelt apology to all I may have offended."

Almost everyone who knew Snyder and had worked with him immediately came to his defense, claiming that in no way, shape, or form was Snyder a racist, and that the statements he made to Hotaling did not reflect his character or beliefs. But it didn't matter if Snyder believed what he said. It didn't matter if he was a racist or not. And it didn't matter if, as he claimed and Ed Hotaling confirmed, Snyder thought he was speaking off the record. It was a terrible thing to say on a day that should have been about celebrating Martin Luther King Jr. and the leaps in progress for which his legacy was responsible. It was, after all, just a year removed from Doug Williams becoming the first black quarterback to start in the Super Bowl.

Instead of pointing to that accomplishment, or to the change in atmosphere around the NFL that was laying the groundwork for Art Shell to be hired a year later as the league's first black head coach, Snyder chose the very low road. While it was clear afterward that he would have given anything to take his words back, as they say, you can't unring the bell.

You can, however, undo a celebrated career in broadcasting. And in 1988 Jimmy "the Greek" Snyder showed us how.

Fools Rush In

September 28, 2003—**Sunday NFL Countdown**

As George Santayana wrote in *The Life of Reason* (later famously paraphrased by Winston Churchill), "Those who cannot remember the past are condemned to repeat it."

I don't know the man and I don't listen to his daily radio program, but I get the impression that Rush Limbaugh is both intelligent and well-read. But he either has never read *The Life of Reason* (no crime there; I don't typically pick up philosophical texts from 1905 either), has never read a book of quotes that included Winston Churchill (less likely), didn't hear about what happened to Jimmy "the Greek" Snyder (extremely doubtful, as he probably commented on the episode on the radio when it happened), or simply didn't care if he repeated history and was therefore condemned for it (where the smart money is).

Rush Limbaugh was hired by ESPN as a pro football commentator in 2003 to a row of raised eyebrows and a chorus of skeptical snickers. Early in his professional life he did work for the Kansas City Royals, but that was long before Limbaugh had built a broadcasting empire as a conservative pundit. Could he really provide good and insightful analysis on ESPN's *Sunday NFL Countdown*? And most important for ESPN, would Limbaugh carry his enormous weekday radio ratings with him to Sunday-morning cable-sports television?

The answer to that question turned out to be a resounding yes. With Limbaugh on board, ESPN's ratings rose by 10 percent overall and 26 percent among the coveted eighteen-to-thirty-four male demographic. And the answer to the first question, regarding his commentary, was also met with positive reviews. He's an intelligent and polished broadcaster, and because of that his learning curve in sports broadcasting was short.

But to no one's surprise the amount of time he could stay away from controversy and just stick to football was also short. Politics and football don't mix. No matter how well articulated you think your point is, the politics of race most certainly don't play well to a mass audience whose main concern on Sunday morning is which number two wide receiver should be in their fantasy football team's starting lineup.

Just four Sundays into the season Limbaugh decided to share his take on the media's relationship with Eagles quarterback Donovan McNabb, saying, "The media has been very desirous that a black quarterback do well. There is a little hope invested in McNabb, and he got a lot of credit for the performance of this team that he didn't deserve. The defense carried this team."

At face value, it wasn't a comment that cut very deep. As a football commentator he had every right to say that he thought McNabb was overrated and that McNabb had the benefit of a great team around him. It was true that McNabb was off to a terrible start in 2003. But he was coming off consecutive trips to the NFC Championship Game and three straight Pro Bowl selections. Unfortunately for him, Limbaugh also added the part about the media and his belief that McNabb was getting a pass because he was black, and that crossed the line that had been highlighted by Jimmy "the Greek" Snyder.

Candidates were gearing up for the 2004 presidential election, so surprise, surprise: Wesley Clark, Howard Dean, and Rev. Al Sharpton immediately called for Limbaugh's firing.

Where there's controversy and a podium, there is a political candidate. And Herbert Lowe, the president of the National Association of Black Journalists, said, "ESPN's credibility as a journalism entity is at stake." (Journalistic credibility? We are talking about ESPN, right? The network of the Nathan's Hot Dog Eating Contest, the World's Strongest Man competition, and Tony Kornheiser?)

Initially the network came to Limbaugh's defense. ESPN executive vice president Mark Shapiro was quoted by *USA Today* saying, "This is not a politically motivated comment. This is a sports and media argument. Rush was arguing McNabb is overrated and that his success is more in part [due] to the team assembled around him."

ESPN did not fire Limbaugh, instead opting to weather the storm. But the clouds of a political controversy multiply like Eagles fans with battery-packed snowballs when the Cowboys are in town. When that controversy was fueled by the hot air of Rush Limbaugh, a lightning rod for the nation's left, this was one tempest that wasn't going to blow itself out.

For each hour that ESPN did not act, the pressure doubled on the network to distance itself from Limbaugh. Finally on the following Wednesday it was Limbaugh who cracked. In a statement issued just before midnight, Limbaugh explained,

> *My comments this past Sunday were directed at the media and were not racially motivated. I offered an opinion. This opinion has caused discomfort with the crew, which I regret.*
>
> *I love* NFL Sunday Countdown *and I do not want to be a distraction to the great work done by all who work on it. Therefore, I have decided to resign.*

There was no word if Limbaugh used his once again free Sunday mornings to read some of the more relevant sections of Santayana's *The Life of Reason.*

Sports Boob
May 11, 1995—LPGA Championship

As a society we have taken our antisexist political correctness beyond the tipping point of reason. Manhole covers officially becoming "maintenance covers" wasn't bad enough. In July of 2008 we officially jumped the shark of appeasement: the city of Atlanta kowtowed to the no doubt crushing pressure placed upon it by *Pink* magazine editor Cynthia Good when it agreed to replace every single one of its "Men at Work" road construction signs with the gender neutral "Workers Ahead." Good raised the issue with city officials after police came to her office on a complaint that she had spray-painted "Wo" on a few of the signs.

The change came at a taxpayer's cost of $144 per sign, because apparently the city has overflowing coffers and absolutely no other problems to solve.

Crime may not pay, but vandalism does. Very bad, Ms. Good.

What's worse, real issues of discrimination get lost in the lunacy. Be it the disreputable auto mechanic who thinks he can take advantage of the single woman with a leaky radiator; the female police officer who is constantly tested on the street by male criminals who refuse to acknowledge her authority; or the female professional athlete who has her achievements and place in the world of sports belittled by the very men paid to cover them.

If you don't remember what CBS golf commentator Ben Wright told reporter Valerie Helmbreck on the opening day of the 1995 LPGA Championship in Wilmington, Deleware, let's refresh the memory. Wright said, "Let's face facts here. Lesbians in the sport hurt women's golf. They are going to a butch game and that furthers the bad image of the game."

He also went on to say that homosexuality on the women's tour "is not reticent. It's paraded. There's a defiance in them."

After adding that the tour's homosexual image scares off some corporate sponsors, he finished up by saying, "Women are handicapped by having boobs. It's not easy for them to keep their left arm straight, and that's one of the tenets of the game. Their boobs get in the way." (One can argue that this is equally a problem for the heavier-set members of the men's tour.)

The next day Helmbreck's story appeared in a Wilmington, Delaware, newspaper, the *News Journal*, and predictably all hell broke loose. There were immediate calls for Wright's firing. Golf took a backseat, with Wright being the only story in town. Everyone was waiting in anticipation for the mea culpa apology and "Sorry, I've become a distraction" resignation that was sure to come.

But not so predictably, especially in light of how executives at CBS reacted in the Jimmy "the Greek" Snyder case, instead of cutting all ties with Wright and issuing their own denunciation of his homophobic and insensitive comments, they came very swiftly and decisively to his defense. David Kenin, the president of CBS Sports, said in a statement, "I am convinced that the offensive statements attributed to Mr. Wright were not made." And Kenin went on to say that "Wright and CBS have been done a grave injustice in this matter."

In defense of himself, Wright wrote, "I am completely disgusted at the pack of lies and distortion that was attributed to me."

And since Helmbreck was from a small newspaper with no actual recording of her conversation with Wright, since CBS was CBS, and since Ben Wright was a well-paid, high-profile national television analyst (plus he spoke with a British accent), he was not fired. The company line had been drawn and that was that. Helmbreck was the villain in this melodrama.

That was where public opinion came to rest—for a while. Six months after talking to Helmbreck, Wright decided to talk to *Sports Illustrated*, and the questions turned to the "pack of lies" that were told in print by the reporter from Delaware. Wright explained to *SI* that Helmbreck was divorced, in a heated child-custody battle, and probably a lesbian herself. And it was just his bad luck to run into her around Mother's Day, when she was particularly unhappy about not being able to see her children. "I was totally misquoted. She put into my mouth words she told me. She's a very unhappy woman."

The big problem with what Wright said, apart from the legal pitfalls he opened himself up to, was that none of it was true. Helmbreck wasn't divorced, there was no custody battle, and no one anywhere in her life could find this alleged ax that she had to grind. As a features writer for the paper she often wrote about food. And when she was asked by *Sports Illustrated* about the things that Wright told her off the record, she refused to reveal them, protecting Wright, even though he had already gone on record calling her a liar.

SI obtained an internal memo that revealed the content of the off-the-record portion of the interview, and it confirmed that she did not use it in her story. The memo referenced what Wright called "the fingernail test"—players with short finger-nails are gay, players with long fingernails are not. With an article from *Sports Illustrated*—not a small-town daily newspaper in Delaware—CBS's indignant denials were no longer worth the paper on which they were written.

Subsequently Wright was no longer working broadcasts for CBS.

It wasn't until three years later that Wright fully came clean, and in the process got a lot of the other players dirty. In May 1998 Wright told *Sports Illustrated* that he was "stupid, naïve, and weak" for following CBS's instructions to deny Helmbreck's quotes. Wright says that he was summoned to the network's headquarters in New York, where executives and lawyers "hammered out a cynical damage-control strategy in which Wright was to deny having made the statement and to discredit Helmbreck."

Wright added, "The most stupid thing I did was remain silent. I should have come out and said, 'Hey, I said all these dumb things, and they were wrong.' I think people would have forgiven me for that."

He called Helmbreck to apologize, and she did forgive him. There were, however, several people who didn't. Most notable among those were the CBS execs he threw under the bus. David Kenin, who had since moved on from CBS, said, "We never told [Wright] to lie or alter any truth." CBS Sports director of communications Leslie Ann Wade said, "Ben Wright's version of the truth is as distorted as it was in 1995."

Whatever the total truth, we will probably never know. But what we can say for sure is that the one person to emerge from this ugliness with integrity firmly attached was small-town reporter Valerie Helmbreck.

Waxing Nostalgic
April 10, 1994—The Masters

There are true sexist comments in sports broadcasting, like Ben Wright's. And there are big-money corporations that will do anything to protect their image and that of their employees, like what CBS is alleged to have done in the wake of the Ben Wright interview.

But not all off-color remarks are created equal. Not all men are insensitive. And sometimes you can overreact to the point that you make yourself look far worse than if you'd just done nothing at all. Such was the case with CBS golf analyst Gary McCord and the collection of uptight, humorless stiffs that run Augusta National Golf Club.

McCord was hired by CBS because of the very fact that he is irreverent. He provides great golf analysis in an entertaining and humorous manner. He is a self-described "smart ass from Southern California" with a quick wit and a disposition to disregard decorum. It is who he is, and he makes no apologies for it. And he shouldn't. It's the very reason why he's been named golf's most popular analyst on multiple occasions.

So when he took the microphone for the first time at The Masters, the powers that be at Augusta knew what they were getting. "That was my shtick," said McCord in an interview with *Golf Magazine*. "I'm going to go in there and be who I am: an absolute idiot."

His shtick played great on television. From the moment the former PGA pro was hired by CBS in 1986, he was an instant hit, injecting life into golf telecasts that were often the favored background noise of the Saturday and Sunday afternoon nap crowd. He was the squawking seagull that broke up the monotony of the "rolling ocean surf" setting on the Tranquil Moments Sleepmate 3000.

But the men—and by men I mean the Colonel Sanders lookalikes with the jocularity of Dick Cheney—who run The Masters are frozen in an eternal nap just one level of consciousness above coma. They hated the squawking seagull, even though they'd initially hired him. So when, in 1994, McCord gave them a good enough reason to get him removed from their beloved annual broadcast of the four most important days in the history of their world, they jumped.

Well, "jumped" might be the wrong word. These fuddy-duddied fossils haven't jumped since the 1920s. They acted. They told CBS that McCord was no longer welcome at Augusta. Because this was The Masters, the crown jewel in CBS Sports' annual golf lineup, CBS execs readily complied.

So what was the thing said by McCord that was so terrible as to get him banned from broadcasting golf's first major tournament every year? There must have been profanities and deep personal insults involved for CBS, which had gone to bat for Ben

Wright, to so willingly show McCord, their number one golf analyst, the Masters door.

Here is what he said while sitting atop the television tower on the 17th: "These greens are so fast they must bikini wax them." Just in case you weren't properly outraged at McCord's insensitivity and wanton disregard for all things decent and sacred, he later quipped that the bumps behind the 17th green resembled "body bags."

Well, firing wasn't enough. It's too good and too tame for the likes of this waggish rogue. Insult women if you want—we know about Augusta's pathetic history when it comes to the fairer sex. Feel free to blast minorities—Augusta National's membership isn't exactly a United Nations of diversity. But don't you dare insult the golf course.

As Tom Weiskopf jokingly put it, "This is Augusta. We do not refer to the flowers as flowers. They are azaleas. They are rosebushes. They are dogwoods. But they can't be flowers, right?"

Showing us why Jack Stephens was never voted "class comic" in high school, the Masters chairman said in a statement, "In prior years we had expressed concern to CBS about the appropriateness of some of Mr. McCord's commentary. In spite of CBS's assurances to the contrary, Mr. McCord's remarks in 1994 were even more distasteful. We therefore felt compelled to seek a change for 1995."

Eddie Elias, McCord's agent, said of the decision, "It's The Masters. What can you do?"

What's troubling is that he was right. The thing that makes The Masters such a great golf tournament is its commitment to the past. Its traditions are like manna from heaven. The Masters of 1948 looks almost exactly like The Masters from 2008. Clearly one of the things that makes The Masters as consistent as a Joe Montana pass, a Tiger Woods tee shot, or the annual "loosening of the teeth" on the infield at Talladega (brought on by its unique mix of rival race fans, short family trees, and a seemingly bottomless trailer's supply of Coors Light) is Augusta National's commitment to stamping out all things funny or clever. They had done this very thing to a CBS commentator before. In 1966 Jack Whitaker was removed from CBS's Masters broadcasting team after he referred to the galleries as "a mob scene."

But the true Mafiosi in this are the men in charge of Augusta who won't tolerate anyone who "goes against the family." Leaving one to wonder if those "body bags" that the handlebar-mustachioed McCord referenced are the buried corpses of the commentators who dared to do so.

Down in the Mouth
Anytime, Anywhere

On occasion the men and women hired to speak learnedly into a microphone about our sports sound like that one college friend who would drunkenly begin authoritatively spouting nonsense about complex subjects he knew nothing about. This is probably as surprising as saying that on the rare occasion politicians will "shape" their principles to match that of the electorate. Shocking, I know.

As a former writer for on-air talent, it was always my job to make the anchor, reporter, or analyst look smart. Fortunately, most of the announcers *were* smart, which made it easy. But repetition can breed complacency, which leads to carelessness, which far too often leads to an impulsive headfirst dive into the uncharted waters of the ad-lib. That is when the masks of the not-so-smart are peeled away, revealing them for mere pretty faces with bleached pearly whites.

When doing an on-camera read that led into a Stanford Cardinal basketball highlight, one such anchor thought it would be clever if he mixed up his proper nouns, and instead of calling the team just "Stanford" or "the Cardinal," he would casually refer to it as "the Redbirds." And that would have been just fine if Stanford was the Cardinals—the bird. It, however, is the Cardinal—the color. Perhaps there are cardinals nesting in the nearly 1,100-year-old El Palo Alto, the redwood tree that is depicted on the Stanford seal. But that is as close to being "the Redbirds" as the university will ever be.

And this was a trained broadcaster with years of on-camera experience. Imagine what happens when you take an athlete and ask him or her to speak extemporaneously for three and a half hours during a game. There is time to kill, minutes upon minutes of potential dead air to fill, and only you and a microphone to do it.

Of course, we don't have to imagine. We are reminded time and time again about the pitfalls that surround our favorite athletes turned broadcasters: athletes hired to be themselves, let their personalities shine, and more important, take us, the viewer or listener, into the dugout, onto the sideline, and inside the heads of the players we cheer for.

You remember what happened to Keith Hernandez, the former National League MVP turned Mets broadcaster. While calling a game in San Diego, Hernandez spotted a woman in the Padres dugout and commented, "Who is the girl in the dugout, with the long hair? You have got to be kidding me. Only player personnel in the dugout." Upon learning that the "girl" in question was Kelly Calabrese, a member of the Padres' training staff, Hernandez didn't back down. "I won't say women belong in the kitchen, but they don't belong in the dugout." He then tried to make it all better by saying, "I'm only teasing. I love you gals out there. I always have."

As per Hernandez's job description, he took us into the mind of a ballplayer.

Then there are the cases of the athlete turned broadcaster who hasn't quite mastered live vs. taped vs. commercial break and the mike is turned off. Former All-Star first baseman Mark Grace, while calling a game for the Diamondbacks and thinking he was talking to the production truck and not the audience, said about catcher Chris Snyder, "Every f——ing swing that guy takes is an underwater swing."

And Bert Blyleven, All-Star pitcher turned Twins broadcaster, unaware that they were doing a live open to a Twins-Yankees broadcast, because they had taped it the two previous games, stopped in the middle of the open and said, "We're going to do this f——ing thing over again because I just f——ed it up."

But accidental slips of the tongue when a broadcaster isn't aware that his comments are being beamed around the country are forgivable. The requisite embarrassment followed by an on-air apology is more than enough to smooth ruffled feathers. Even in the case of Neanderthal Keith Hernandez, we accepted his apology. (It probably didn't hurt him any that he had been on *Seinfeld*.)

Sometimes, however, a broadcaster goes so far over the line that a simple apology and reprimand is hardly enough to undo his deeds.

ESPN analyst Rick Sutcliffe stopped by the booth during a Padres-Brewers game in May 2006 on one of his days off. Considering that he had been drinking, somewhat heavily, with actor Bill Murray earlier in the day on the golf course, Sutcliffe would have been far better served to have stayed away.

Upon getting to an open microphone, the rambling Sutcliffe immediately launched into a story about his daughter and her upcoming trip to Africa, saying, "How about that? Over there on one of those missions, man. George Clooney—you been seeing that? Yeah, he's up there with the Congress, he's trying to get everyone to solve that thing."

Sutcliffe was referencing George Clooney's efforts on behalf of Darfur, which was a strange and out of place meander considering that this was a baseball broadcast. But it was harmless, if not for the fact that he was obviously intoxicated. But Sutcliffe went beyond the line of no harm, no foul when he began to pester play-by-play man Matt Vasgersian about his current choice of an employer—which was incidentally the network where the conversation was taking place.

"Matty, what are you still doing here in San Diego?"

Vasgersian gamely tried to turn the conversation back to the game at hand, but Sutcliffe would have none of it.

"No, no, no, Matty. Everybody on Earth has been trying to steal you—the Dodgers, the Cubs, ESPN. What are you still doing *here?*"

After an apology the next day Sutcliffe was suspended by ESPN for one game.

The worst of the bunch, however, was Miami Hurricanes color commentator Lamar Thomas, himself a former University of Miami football player. In 2006 Miami and crosstown rival Florida International got embroiled in one of the worst bench-clearing brawls ever seen in college football. While the fight raged on the field, only to end after the Miami-Dade County police were called on to restore order several minutes later, Thomas went from broadcaster to wannabe brawler:

Now, that's what I'm talking about! You come into our house, you should get your behind kicked! You don't come into the OB [Orange Bowl] playing that stuff. You can't come over to our place talking noise like that. You'll get your butt beat. I was about to go down the elevator to get in that thing. I say, why don't we meet outside the tunnel after the ball game and get it on some more? You don't come into the OB, baby. Not in our house!

Thirty-two players were suspended for one game (a mere slap on the wrist) and the thirty-six-year-old Lamar Thomas was fired (rightly).

The moral of these tales is simple. Always stick to the script. And when there isn't one, always broadcast with a seven-second delay.

Lost in Translation
August 1–17, 2003—Pan American Games

Anyone who has ever taken a foreign language in school understands that there is no such thing as an automatic translation into English. Sometimes the words match and it works. And sometimes it doesn't. The German phrase *Meine Grossmutter führt die neue Tankstelle* matches up perfectly word for word with its English translation: "My grandmother manages the new gas station." But the Spanish phrase *Trabajé un mes para cultivar este bigote* flip-flops the first two words of its English counterpart, translating directly as "Worked I a month to grow this mustache."

Along with actually memorizing the ever-so-useful phrases that you learn in [insert your favorite foreign language] 101, coming to terms with the inconsistency of translation is the biggest hurdle to mastering a new language and using it with native speakers while traveling abroad. Well, that and finding a mustached man who has a gas-station-managing grandmother.

Thanks to inconsistencies and exceptions, there is no easy, automatic way to translate one language to another. Yet for some reason computer-generated word replacers continue to get made and tried—and always with incredibly comical results.

The American Family Association is one of a number of organizations that has decided that it has the right to change the language of secondary source stories that it then presents to its members. It often takes stories from the Associated Press, edits the content to make them more AFA acceptable, and then places them on its own news website, OneNewsNow.com. It also makes these changes without making any notations that it is doing so.

But editing the hundreds of dailies that are churned out by the Associated Press can be time consuming, especially when all you're really looking for is a few objectionable words. For example, the word "gay," which the AFA finds ambiguous. Why not just have a computer automatically replace the word "gay" with the word "homosexual" each time it finds it in a story?

Here's why. Because there is a U.S. Olympic sprinter named Tyson Gay. And when Gay advanced to the finals of the U.S. Olympic Trials in 2008, the headline, as seen on OneNewsNow. com, read "Homosexual Eases into 100 Final at Olympic Trials."

The absurdity of the AFA was only deepened in the opening few paragraphs:

> *Tyson Homosexual easily won his semifinal for the 100 meters at the U.S. Olympic track and field trials. . . . On Saturday Homosexual misjudged the finish in his opening heat and had to scramble to finish fourth. . . . Asked how he felt, Homosexual said: "A little fatigued."*

This came just two days after the AP referenced NBA player Rudy Gay in a story about a Grizzlies-Timberwolves trade. Oh, the homosexual horror.

But perhaps the funniest example of a computer program gone awry happened when the 2003 Pan American Games were held in the Dominican Republic, and automatic language-translating software was used to take the original Spanish-language stories and translate them into English. The games' official website utilized the translating software Babel Fish. When fans from English-speaking nations logged onto the website to see results and read stories and recaps, this is what they saw:

To the compass of merengue and samba, the Pan-American Games of Santo Domingo lowered to Sunday their drop curtain, shouting to all lung of which it knew to be to the height of a sport joust of great profile.

And this:

The closing ceremony was a waste of music and fireworks, in which Santo Domingo passed the slug to Rio de Janeiro, the seat of the games of the 2007.

And the best of them all:

The successes of Cuba in the Pan-American Games of Santo Domingo are been from kindness of the social system of the island, according to Fidel I castrate. "Our revolution has created the ideal conditions. We will be in a tenth floor having begun by the cellar," said I castrate during a speech Wednesday at night, shortly before starting off for Paraguay.

If Hollywood has taught us anything with its slew of futuristic cautionary tales, such as *2001: A Space Odyssey, Alien,* and *The Terminator,* it's this: computers cannot be trusted.

Have we learned nothing?

POTPOURRI

Even though a Super Bowl–winning team has only forty-five players on its active roster for the season's final Sunday, the number of diamond-laden Super Bowl rings that get passed out the following season can be close to three hundred. Trainers, equipment managers, front-office staff (marketing, ticket sales, etc.), and almost any other full- and part-time employees get the gift as an acknowledgment that their contributions, however anonymous, played a part in bringing home the title.

Some teams even go a little above and beyond in expressing their gratitude to the scores of sports professionals who work behind the scenes. When the Chicago White Sox won the World Series in 2005 they gave out 432 rings and 163 pendants—including on their list past Hall of Famers like Carlton Fisk (who hadn't played for the Sox since 1993) and the families of past owners, including Charlie Comiskey's clan, who hadn't owned a stake in the team since 1961, and John Allyn's family, despite Allyn's majority ownership ending in 1975 with exactly zero postseason appearances in fourteen years of leadership.

But in the paraphrased words of Spider-Man's Uncle Ben,

"With even a modicum of power comes great responsibility." In the world of sports, often the responsibility is for a loss. Or worst of all, the loss of a championship.

The ancillary figures in sports don't make multimillions from having a facsimile of their signature stamped on the side of a sneaker. You, as a fan, have never burned to buy an authentic autographed jersey of your favorite team's head groundskeeper. But a bonehead decision by one of these men or women can just as easily send your team on the road to ruination as a botched 3rd-down call or a pitching change that came one batter too late.

For coaches and players the opportunities for imbecility are as numerous as the length of their careers allow. They are always under the watchful eye of supporters desperate to cheer, ready to boo, and always poised to criticize. But for the forgotten fomenters in sports, including friends, family, and even fans, the occasions for infamy are as rare as the flowering titan arum (better known as the corpse flower). And the stench they've left on the world of sports is every bit as pungent.

Man-eating Tarp
October 13, 1985—NLCS Game 4, Dodgers vs. Cardinals

We've all seen the replay of a hobbling Kirk Gibson, playing through awful knee pain, driving Dennis Eckersley's 3-2 2-out pitch over the wall in right field for an improbable 1988 Game 1 World Series win. And we've all heard about the legend of Jack Youngblood playing in both the NFC Championship Game and Super Bowl XIV on a broken left leg, in the ultimate display of "sports warrior."

This is not one of those stories.

The history of bizarre injuries in sports is as rich a tapestry as the history of the sports themselves. Rockies shortstop Clint

After getting run over by Busch Stadium's automatic tarp before Game 4 of the NLCS, Cardinals rookie Vince Coleman, the fastest man in baseball every other day of the 1985 season, is carried off the field. Also on the stretcher were the Cardinals' hopes of a World Series title. *(© Bettmann/Corbis)*

Barmes would like to be remembered for his stellar rookie season in 2005. Instead, he will always be the guy who missed three months, and perhaps lost the Rookie of the Year Award, because of a broken collarbone . . . sustained while carrying deer meat up the stairs.

Terry Mulholland, a former All-Star starting pitcher and twenty-year veteran of Major League Baseball, pitched in fifteen career postseason games and in 1986 recorded the first no-hitter in Veterans Stadium history. But he is also, and forever will be, the guy who missed a game after he scratched his right eyeball by rolling over an errant feather let loose from a hotel pillow.

Soccer goalie Lionel Letizi once threw out his back while stretching to pick up a dropped Scrabble tile. NHL goalie Glenn Healy cut his catching hand while cleaning his bagpipes. And the Sacramento Kings lost Lionel Simmons for two games in the 1990–91 season because of wrist tendonitis brought on by excessive play of his Nintendo Game Boy.

But in terms of the way an injury impacted the results on the field—and the annals of the "absolutely preventable" and "never should have happened"—nothing compares to the case of Vince Coleman and the man-eating Busch Stadium tarpaulin.

Coleman began the 1985 season in the minor leagues. Despite his stealing 145 bases in AA ball in 1983 and another 101 in 1984 at AAA Louisville, the Cardinals thought the speedy left fielder needed a little more seasoning before he'd make an impact in the big leagues. That extra seasoning lasted a total of nine games, when injuries to Willie McGee and Tito Landrum forced St. Louis to promote the twenty-three-year-old and insert him in the starting lineup—a place he never left. His impact was so immediate that the Cardinals were content to trade their opening day starting left fielder, Lonnie Smith, by mid-May.

So by the time the afternoon of October 13 rolled around, Vince Coleman was a household name. He had shattered the rookie stolen base record with 110 successful swipes (Tim Raines had held the record with 71 in 1981), he was the unanimous runaway winner of the Rookie of the Year Award, and his Cardinals were the favorites to win the World Series following a 101-win regular season. In a matter of a few short months Vince Coleman had become baseball's fastest-rising star.

Only to be undone by a falling barometer and an inattentive grounds crew.

Shortly after 5:00 p.m., just a couple of hours before the start of Game 4 of the NLCS and with the Cardinals scattered around the diamond for their turn at batting practice, rain started to fall in St. Louis. And because keeping a dry infield was paramount to the success of the small-ball-playing Cards, the grounds crew acted swiftly and decisively. While one crew team tackled the task of breaking down the batting cage and clearing the infield of errant balls and the protective barriers set up at first base and on the mound, another group activated Busch Stadium's state-of-the-art automatic tarp.

At one end of the 1,200-pound, motor-driven aluminum cylinder was its operator, controlling the machinery from short right field. At the other end, near home plate, making his way back to the Cardinals' dugout without the slightest inkling of the bizarre accident to come, was baseball's fastest man.

It happened in a split second. One moment Coleman was tossing his glove to pitching coach Dave Ricketts, still standing on the first-base side of the tarp. The next, the tarp had caught his left foot—a foot that had routinely taken him the 90 feet from first to second base at more than 20 miles an hour—and as he tried to get away it knocked him to the ground and began to roll up his leg. It rolled up his ankle and made it as high as midthigh before the shouting of his teammates registered with the operator, who then quickly reversed the machine off of the most valuable legs in the city.

But it was too late. The damage had been done.

Initially the team physician, Dr. Stanley London, said the injury did not appear to be serious and announced to the relieved Redbirds that X-rays were negative. He even said that there was a chance that Coleman would only miss that night's game.

But one game stretched to another, and after the Cardinals rallied to win four straight over LA and advance to the World Series, St. Louis was still without its leadoff hitter. Eight days after the incident, and with the Cardinals up 2–0 over Kansas City, "the key" to the Cardinals National League pennant, as described by pitcher Joaquin Andujar, was ruled out for the rest of the Series. A tiny bone chip—less than 3 millimeters wide—had been discovered on the outside part of his bruised left knee.

Tito Landrum did a more-than-adequate job of filling in for the injured Coleman. He got four hits in his emergency start in Game 4, finishing the NLCS with a .429 batting average. And in the World Series Landrum's bat stayed hot as he hit .360 with a home run. But, as infamously known, the Cardinals ended up losing the controversial World Series to the Royals in seven games.

In my previous book, *The Worst Call Ever!*—the unquestioned authoritative voice regarding all things bad umpires and referees have wrought—the Cardinals' series-ending collapse is blamed on umpire Don Denkinger. But without Coleman, the man who had been setting the table for the St. Louis offense all season long, the Cardinals managed to score just 13 runs in seven games. Twice they scored just 1 run in games at home, and they were shut out completely in the decisive Game 7, scattering five singles over nine innings and never threatening to plate a run. Without their top speedster, the team that had stolen a league-high 314 bases during the regular season managed to pilfer just two bags against their I-70 rivals.

In St. Louis the anger aimed at Denkinger is still palpable more than two decades later. But an offending party who never fully shared the blame for the Cardinals' postseason perdition, and to this day remains anonymous in the history books, was one of St. Louis's own—the grounds crew's shamefully incompetent tarp controller.

BS BCS

1998 to Not Soon Enough—NCAA Bigwigs

The history of the world is littered with discarded and discredited bad ideas. Even the pillars of creativity and ingenuity are not immune to error. Remember New Coke and Crystal Pepsi?

Spray-on hair, thong underwear for men, and Mia Farrow's decision to adopt Soon-Yi were all at one time considered solid strokes of genius. But when viewed in the glare of 20/20 hindsight, not so much.

I, however, am not nearly feeling as charitable toward the lamebrains who concocted the Bowl Championship Series as a means of deciding the NCAA Division I-A (Football Bowl Subdivision, or FBS, for the five of you who call it that) national football championship "on the field." It never had its day. It was never a good idea. And it never had a chance of doing what was intended—assuming that the intent was to crown a true national champion. If the intent was to make huge wads of cash for the already super-rich television networks and athletic conferences, then bravo. Well done on that front, BCS frauds.

The pro-BCS crowd don't so much as defend their system— a system that keeps the power of deciding a national champion away from the players actually fighting for the title—but instead give you all the reasons why a playoff would be bad. So let's examine those.

The favored argument of the NCAA presidents is academics. Adding weeks to the season will, according to them, take points off a player's GPA. Think of all the missed classes.

Really? Do these guys miss class during the regular season? A regular season that has now stretched into twelve games because it means more revenue, and, in many conferences, a season that is only decided with a championship game (a form of playoff) that has teams playing a thirteenth game *before* bowl season even starts?

No one is suggesting that a playoff take place on a different day of the week. Stick with Saturday, when there are *no* classes— just like in September, October, and November, when the students have always been able to attend class, practice, and play the game. These things aren't mutually exclusive.

And that brings up another giant hole in the academics argument. A playoff would take place in late December/early January, when, as luck would have it, every college in the nation is off. LSU, the BCS champion for the 2007 regular season, finished final exams for its fall semester on December 15 and didn't begin spring classes until January 14. That's a full month off.

So what classes, exactly, will a limited playoff system keep these student-athletes from attending? In March, smack dab in the middle of everyone's semester, sixty-four college basketball teams (plus thirty-two NIT teams) play games in the middle of the week. And that usually follows several midweek games played in a conference tournament. Why don't the stewards of academic integrity cry foul for them?

The next time one of these blowhard university presidents starts droning on about a playoff hurting these fine young men's academic future, mock and ridicule them mercilessly.

Another crutch BCS supporters like to lean on when their omnipotent authority is challenged is the "it will destroy the integrity of the bowl system" defense. Again, I say, "Really?" Exactly which bowl's integrity are you concerned about? The Chuck E. Cheese Munch N' Play Mozzarella Stick Bowl? Or the Mercury Auto Insurance Mechanical Breakdown Bowl?

You wouldn't want to miss out on the excitement of Florida Atlantic and Memphis playing in front of 23,000 screaming fans. And if you could channel the electricity created by the Rutgers–Ball State grudge match (with their identically impressive 7-5 records) at the 2008 International Bowl (since when did a separation of 650 miles and two states constitute "international"?) you might be able to toast two slices of bread, lightly.

The BCS already tells me that only four bowls matter. And of those four, only one *really* matters. Everything else is just a showy made-for-TV event that has no bearing on the conventional reason for a postseason, the awarding of a championship. The real deciders of who may lay claim to the title is a collection of balding overweight sportswriters who are biased toward the teams and conferences they cover and the small handful of games that they are actually able to see. These men, with their high cholesterol and Cheetos-stained fingernails, are the masters of the college football universe, not the bowls.

And finally, the last firewall of the BCS lobbyist is the "a play-off will diminish the most exciting regular season in sports" assertion. Well, don't you believe it.

The regular season in college football is great. And each win is incredibly meaningful. But losses are judged as much by the opponent as by the calendar. Again, look at LSU's championship season in 2007. Each of the top-6 teams in the AP's final top-25 poll had two losses, including LSU. The team that finished ranked seventh, Kansas, had only one. The problem was that Kansas's loss came on the final week of the season. Because the Jayhawks have no football history (outside of Gale Sayers), they started off the season unranked. As the 13-0 Auburn Tigers of 2004 can attest, if you begin the season with a low preseason ranking it too often doesn't matter what happens on the field. If the hole is too big, you can't ever climb out. History and expectations, or a lack of either, are just as important as wins and losses in deciding who finishes atop the polls.

The fact is, if you had an eight-team playoff, still using the current BCS bowls for your four first-round matchups if you'd like, no one is getting in with more than two losses. And in most college football seasons, two losses will often be enough to keep you out. That still places an incredibly high premium on the regular season. With a playoff, and thus a way to rescue your national championship hopes in the face of one down week, we would probably see an uptick in high-profile early season matchups. USC and Oklahoma would no longer have to avoid each other like the plague in September, fearful that a loss will derail their entire season. Teams could venture beyond the Montana States and Western Carolinas and actually play games within the top 25.

A playoff system would create no more than a handful of extra games for a very select few teams. Sure, if you make it an eight-team playoff, No. 9 is going to complain. Make it twelve teams, and No. 13 is going to feel slighted. But you can be pretty confident that at the very least, the best team in the country has been included in the tournament. At that point, if the teams can't take care of it on the field, they have no one to blame but themselves.

In the final AP top-25 poll following the 2007 season, four different teams received first-place votes, including three for No. 2 Georgia. If Georgia, according to the brainiacs who have more say on who gets to play for the title than everyone else, truly is the second-best team in the land, is it fair that they never got to face LSU on the field? Ohio State, deemed worthy of that championship shot by the sportswriters, finished fifth—also according to the sportswriters.

Tell me again how that's better than a playoff.

Juicing the Bottom Line
Summer of 1998 to ???—Major League Baseball

Steroid use in baseball predates the summer of 1998, of course. The late Ken Caminiti admitted to using steroids during his NL MVP season of 1996, estimating to *Sports Illustrated* that half of all big-league ballplayers were using at the time. Convicted steroid dealer Kirk Radomski told investigators working for former senator George Mitchell that he sold steroids that same year to Mets catcher Todd Hundley. Hundley, with a previous career high of 16 home runs, hit 41 in 1996. He received a $2.32 million raise the following season.

Baseball's steroid past is as long as one of Jose Canseco's upper-deck home runs after he shoots a triple cocktail of

On March 17, 2005, Sammy Sosa, Mark McGwire, Rafael Palmeiro, and Curt Schilling testified before the congressional committee investigating steroid use in baseball. Four and a half months later, after defiantly denying to Congress that he ever used steroids, Palmeiro tested positive. *(Win McNamee/Getty Images)*

Deca-Durabolin, Equipoise, and HGH. In an interview with *San Francisco Chronicle* reporter Ron Kroichick, former pitcher Tom House admitted to using steroids during his playing days in the 1970s. He also told Kroichick, as detailed in a 2005 *Chronicle* article titled "House a 'Failed Experiment' with Steroids," that use was widespread among baseball pitching staffs throughout the '60s and '70s and involved human growth hormone and "steroids they wouldn't give to horses." It was, and still is, the earliest account of steroid use in baseball.

Steroid history has also been filled with moments every bit as hypocritical as one of Canseco's so-called tell-all books in which he outs his fellow players for their steroid use because in the end all he really cares about is the good of the game. Which is just as gag-inducing as when Commissioner Bud Selig says, "It's not like we've ignored the problem" (actual statement) or, my personal favorite, "I never even heard about it."

The unofficial head-buried-in-the-sand policy actually predates Selig and the summer of 1998. But it was that season, when Sammy Sosa and Mark McGwire began their assault on Roger Maris's single-season home-run record, when baseball officially sold its moneymaking soul to the steroid devil.

The sport did its best to commit suicide in 1994 when a bunch of really rich guys decided that instead of reaching a compromise that would keep them all in mansions, yachts, and a tax bracket most men dare not dream of, they would cancel the World Series. Baseball and the Fall Classic had survived the Black Sox scandal of 1919, four summers of fighting Nazi Germany, Pete Rose's gambling saga and subsequent banishment, and the hot-weather uniforms the White Sox sported in 1976 that featured Bermuda-length navy shorts and collared white pullover tops. Yet in 1994 the resiliency of our National Pastime was no match for the three most dreaded words in professional sports: collective bargaining agreement.

It was almost baseball's death blow. The Yankees' reemergence as a power in 1996 helped stave off the reading of the last rites. But overall attendance in 1997 was still down 10 percent from the prestrike high of 70 million in 1993, and television ratings were sinking. American kids were playing soccer, watching Michael Jordan lead his Bulls to a second NBA championship three-peat, and pretending to be Barry Sanders in their backyards. Baseball was becoming an afterthought.

Then, out of the darkness, came light. From the shadows at the edge of the abyss rode two white horses mounted by a pair of statuesque saviors carrying dueling hammers of Thor. When the 1998 chase of Roger Maris was born, thanks to these two redeemers of the RBI, protectors of the pennant, and caretakers of Cracker Jack, baseball was saved.

When Sammy Sosa or Mark McGwire hit a home run that summer, it didn't just lead the sports section, it often led the news. Programming was interrupted with breaking news: McGwire just hit number 50. Live coverage whisked us out to Wrigley Field for Sosa's 56th. And when the first week of September rolled around, and as luck would have it the Cubs were visiting the Cardinals, no one was talking about the upcoming NFL or college football seasons. All eyes were on baseball.

You know the rest. Roger Maris's record was shattered by two players in the same season. Then, the very next year, both McGwire and Sosa broke 61 again. This after the record of 61 stood for thirty-seven years. In the previous fifty years only once did someone hit as many as 60 home runs—and that was Maris.

McGwire and Sosa are not "known" to have used steroids. But allegations have swirled around Sosa for years, and he was mentioned in a federal affidavit related to the Mitchell investigation. When he was found to be using a corked bat in 2003 his credibility dropped like a stone . . . not unlike the plummeting opinion of McGwire after he evaded questions before Congress about steroid use. The onetime lock to be a first-ballot Hall of Famer received just 23.5 percent of the vote in 2007, his first year of eligibility.

Again, in the words of Bud Selig, "It's not like we've ignored the problem."

No, Bud, you didn't ignore the problem. You gave it a giant hug of gratitude. Because what ticket-buying fan and television network executive doesn't love the home run? And you weren't about to quibble with what was right when that was tantamount to biting the hand that was feeding you caviar served on a silver platter.

Since Selig took over the reins of baseball by successfully ousting Fay Vincent from the commissioner's job in 1992, he has been incredibly shortsighted. Remember contraction? Even though throwing the steroid blinders on during the beginning of the home-run boom revived interest in baseball and helped pave the way for a series of new ballparks (twelve new stadiums opened in the ten years following McGwire's 62nd home run), like all gluttons, Selig and baseball would eventually be undone by their own myopic greed. When BALCO-ed Barry Bonds (you can't have a steroid story without mentioning him) was chasing Hank Aaron's record for most career home runs, all the excitement of 1998 had been replaced with anger and contempt. Then came the Mitchell Report, with names like Roger Clemens and his guaranteed spot in Cooperstown. And just like that baseball was back to 1994.

Baseball is as much if not more about its history than it is about its present. And yet its present caretakers seem to care nothing for the past. So why should the fans care?

Baseball will, of course, survive. As a rich tapestry of American history, it will endure because ultimately we all want it to. But when it emerges from the steroid shadows, weakened and wounded, the history books will not be kind. Because, to be sure, this time these wounds are entirely self-inflicted.

Assault with a Deadly Wife
July 1, 1995—Wimbledon Third Round,
Jeff Tarango vs. Alexander Mronz

If you are a man and married, no doubt you have at one time or another felt emasculated by your wife. Be it her leaning across the table at dinner to wipe an undetected chili smear from your chin; her convincing you that "real men" do get mani-pedis— only to result in an afternoon of you sitting sheepishly in the pedicure chair while dealing with the internal tug-of-war over your embarrassment at being the spa's only male customer and the absolute tranquillity brought on by a heavenly foot soak (generic example that has no personal relation to me); or being forced to buy your wife, Vanessa, an 8-karat diamond ring and the world's only automatic converted Lamborghini Murciélago after publicly declaring that she's "the air" you breathe because you were forced to admit adultery (also a generic example and any similarities to actual persons is purely coincidental).

These examples of marital emasculation, of course, all come with happy endings. Who doesn't want a food-free face, soft-as-a-baby's-butt feet, or a placated wife and mother-in-law who is rumored to be more than a little demanding? But what if your wife showed up at your workplace, decided you were being treated badly by your boss, and slapped him? That might be a little harder to get over.

That is exactly what happened to American Jeff Tarango at Wimbledon in 1995.

Wimbledon has had a strange and storied history. There have been numerous streakers over the years—even on days when the royal box sat empty. During World War II it was bombed by the Germans and 1,200 seats at Centre Court were destroyed. And in 1995, thanks to Tarango and his incredibly short temper, a Frenchman was attacked by a crazed Frenchwoman, delighting scores of Londoners.

The Frenchman in question was chair umpire Bruno Rebeuh. The Frenchwoman was Tarango's wife, Benedicte. But the incident that day at the All England Lawn Tennis Club actually began to take root back in 1993. That is when Tarango claims to have overheard two women having a conversation with Rebeuh at a cocktail party regarding how the umpire shows favoritism to certain players in exchange for their friendship. Tarango then made the allegation to tennis official Gilbert Yserne, who, Tarango claims, privately agreed that if Tarango would keep his allegations out of the official record, Rebeuh would never chair another of Tarango's matches.

Again, it should be noted, that all of this is according to Tarango, in allegations made only after he was kicked out of Wimbledon in 1995.

The incident that day began when Tarango, repeatedly upset by Rebeuh's rulings throughout his match with Alexander Mronz, became particularly incensed by an out call on a serve that cost him game point. Complaining vocally during the changeover, Tarango began to get booed by some in the crowd, for which he shouted, "Shut up, [blank]!" Rebeuh then issued a verbal-abuse warning for uttering an audible obscenity, which prompted Tarango to demand that a supervisor replace Rebeuh on the spot.

When the supervisor refused, an angry Tarango gathered up his rackets, packed up his bags, and stormed off the court, yelling to Rebeuh, "You are the most corrupt official in the game. I'm not playing anymore!"

And just in case that boorish behavior wasn't embarrassing enough, as Rebeuh made his way back to the umpire's changing room he was chased down by Benedicte Tarango, who promptly slapped him across the face. Later, when she was asked why she had done it, Benedicte's less-than-contrite reply was, "Well, if Jeff had done it, he would have been put out of tennis. The guy deserves a lesson."

In addition to his sportsmanship, Jeff's apologizing skills could also use some work. After the prerequisite cooling-off period, Tarango said of Rebeuh, "I think the guy's a loser." He then proudly told his wife, "I'm glad you did that."

Both Tarangos were told to stay away from Wimbledon the following year.

For the record, the tournament referee that year in Wimbledon, Alan Mills, denied any knowledge of the previous feud between Tarango and Rebeuh. "I personally have never heard of the allegations against Bruno from this particular player. He is acknowledged as one of the finest chair umpires in the world."

It has since been widely acknowledged that Jeff and Benedicte

Tarango are one of the worst mixed-doubles pairs to ever soil the grounds at Wimbledon.

A Mother's Work Is Never Done
September 21, 1989—Tony Wilson vs. Steve McCarthy

As best illustrated in the long-running sitcom *Seinfeld*, mothers will always be there to defend their children. When typical mom Helen Seinfeld heard that Crazy Joe Davola didn't like her son, Jerry, she immediately asked, "How can anyone not like you? You're a wonderful, wonderful boy. Everybody likes you. It's impossible not to like you." Speaking like a true father, Morty Seinfeld responded, "Maybe some people don't like him. I could see that."

I suppose this could be the reason why when most athletes find themselves isolated on camera after a big hit, goal, or touchdown, the first words out of their mouth are "Hi, Mom." Because in your mother's eyes, you can never do wrong. And if anyone tries to tell her otherwise, well, then that person becomes her sworn enemy.

I certainly felt the wrath of many mothers when I was a Little League umpire for a summer. How dare I, the big, bad, mean umpire, call her son out on strikes? If he didn't swing at the pitch, then it's because it was a ball. Who did I think I was to question his finely tuned nine-year-old batting eye? What kind of overgrown ogre must I be to officiate her son's mercy-rule-shortened 17-run defeat? Never mind the fact that I was only fifteen myself.

The great thing about this blind protection that mothers cloak over their children (or bad thing, if you live within a certain radius of Mom) is that no matter how old you get, the instinct never goes away. As proof, I submit my own mother, who is, right at this very minute, waiting to hear that this book has been added to Oprah's Book Club while simultaneously a Hollywood bidding war has broken out to secure the television and film rights. Because really, how can anyone not like me?

For the most part Mom's love is harmless. It makes her happy, so no reason to get fussed. Except in the rare instance when Mom finds herself ringside at a boxing match in which her beloved baby boy was just knocked to the canvas by the brutish thug in opposing trunks. Imagine you're teasing a baby bear cub when Mamma Grizzly shows up and you can probably picture the scene in the third round of the Tony Wilson–Steve McCarthy fight in September of 1989.

In a fight for the British light-heavyweight championship, McCarthy got in the first big blow of the night when he knocked Wilson to the mat in the third round, leading to a mandatory 8-count. As the referee applied the count to the stunned Wilson and McCarthy regrouped in the opposite corner, Wilson's mother, Minna, climbed into the ring and began to pummel McCarthy with her high-heeled shoe.

Eventually security came to the aid of the unbeaten McCarthy, but not before Mother Wilson had opened a cut on his head that required four stitches to close. Then, when McCarthy refused to continue the bout because of the cut and subsequent medical condition, the British referees awarded the win to Wilson. Tony Wilson, that is.

Recognizing that something didn't seem right about a mother providing the knockout blow for her professional boxer son's match for the title, the British Boxing Board of Control met to discuss the matter. And in their infinite wisdom the board ruled that the Wilson victory would stand despite "the unsatisfactory nature of the ending of this contest." But they did order that a rematch would have to be fought, and it would have to be done without Minna Wilson's attendance.

That was just fine with Minna Wilson, who told reporters, "I will never go back to one of his fights."

Tony Wilson would have ten more fights in his career. None of them were the required rematch with Steve McCarthy after a bout with the flu forced McCarthy to withdraw from a scheduled fight two months after he was felled by the high heel. And none of those ten fights took place with Mother Wilson watching from the crowd.

Play My Boy or Else
October 22, 2006—Oxford Circle Raiders vs. Burholme Outlaws

In the life of a child there is no substitute for a good parent. Nothing learned through books, from teachers, or with their peers can compete in importance with the path set for a child's life by a parent's deeds and words. That's the good news for parents who are desperately trying to cancel out the influences of MTV's and VH-1's continuing competition to drain the final few ounces of water out of the world's shallowest pool of television programming (Spencer and Heidi—why tigers eat their young), Britney Spears, and *High School Musical*—don't get me started.

It also happens to be the bad news for the many therapists who will spend years of lengthy, tear-filled couch sessions trying to undo the damage that the ever-growing population of parental nut jobs is doing to said children.

From the five-year-old who swears like a trucker after hearing dear old Dad shout at the TV every NFL Sunday afternoon (exactly the reason I don't have kids), to the parent who boils with road rage during carpool every time he gets stuck behind a tourist in a wood-paneled PT Cruiser with a "searching for satellite" TomTom, to the well-meaning parents who want so badly to see their child achieve her dreams that they hatch a plot to murder the rival cheerleader's mother, we've all seen— or been—them.

Of course, Wanda Holloway, the "Texas Cheerleader-Murdering Mom," is an extreme case. The solicitation of capital murder by an overenthused soccer mom is the exception, not the rule. But even the most mild-mannered of parents can get heated when it comes to his child's athletic endeavors. Perhaps you read about the March 2008 story of Larry King (yes, that Larry King) allegedly getting into a confrontation with a Beverly Hills Little League umpire. The seventy-four-year-old King was a volunteer coach for his nine-year-old's Little League team (if there is anyone who knows how to toss a softball, it's King) and King thought that his septuagenarian eyes and Hubble Space Telescope–thick eyeglasses afforded him a better view of the call than the umpire's.

The incident ended with King being banished to the deepest recesses of the outfield as a mere spectator. Thankfully, heads cooled before there was any suspender snapping or threats by King to "marry [the umpire's] wife right now." (Philadelphia, hello! Go, caller.)

And that, in a very roundabout and intentional way, takes us to the case of Philadelphia father Wayne Derkotch.

October 22, 2006, was your typical fall Sunday morning in the City of Brotherly Love. The Eagles were playing later that afternoon, so somewhere in South Philly a fan was booing in preparation. Ryan Howard had recently finished his MVP year with the Phillies by hitting 58 home runs, and someone was calling in to WIP Sports Radio to blast Howard as a "bum." And large men with 36-inch waistlines and over throughout the city were taking their morning dose of Lipitor and chasing it with a jumbo hoagie or cheese steak loaded with Whiz.

Meanwhile, Wayne Derkotch was in Northeast Philadelphia watching his son's Burholme Outlaws do battle with the Oxford Circle Raiders while packing a .357 Magnum. As everyone would later find out, Derkotch did have a permit to carry. But why he chose to carry a gun so powerful that it is the preferred pistol of Inspector "Dirty" Harry Callahan to a peewee football game between six- and seven-year-olds defies explanation. As does his decision to pull it.

As the story goes, according to eyewitnesses who passed on the info to Philadelphia police, Derkotch was upset by the fact that his son was sitting on the bench. He began to argue with fill-in coach Jermaine Wilson about why his son wasn't in the game. That argument escalated into a scuffle, which ballooned into a full-blown fight, and when the 5-foot-9 Derkotch began to feel that the 6-foot-3 Wilson was getting the better of him, he pulled out his equalizer, the .357.

"Everyone started screaming, 'Gun! Gun!'" said referee Shawn Henwood. "I told all the kids, 'Run, go that way.' I herded them all to the other side of the field. They were screaming. It was nuts. Mothers were grabbing their children, you know, trying to protect them and shield them. It was horrible."

As chaos broke loose on the field, Derkotch, using the cover of a pointed and loaded weapon, made his way back to his car. And Henwood, thinking that Derkotch was trying to escape the scene that he had created, went over to write down Derkotch's license-plate number. That started a fight between him and Derkotch's brother, which clearly the referee won when the brother was arrested and charged with assault.

Derkotch, as a Philadelphia judge would find, was not trying to flee the scene. He was going to wait for police in the relative safety of his car. Although one might contend that as the only one armed for the Outlaws-Raiders Sunday-morning grudge match (it was the Raiders, after all), he could have been safe waiting it out on the 50-yard line.

It was also found by that judge that Derkotch was acting in self-defense, never mind the fact that he started the fight. And it was argued that Derkotch only pulled the gun when, in the words of defense attorney Brian Quinn, "He was in fear of dying." The judge bought that as well, swallowing the defense's claim that of all the adults there that Sunday, Derkotch was the one who acted "responsibly." Seriously.

Charges of aggravated assault, simple assault, and reckless endangerment were all dropped. But Derkotch won't get off scot-free. He'll be on the hook for bail the first time his boy has a "like father, like son" moment with a gun. The clock is ticking.

Count Your Blessings . . . and Your Clubs
July 22, 2001—British Open Final Round

As far as Ian Woosnam is concerned, Albert Einstein got it wrong when he said, "Everything that can be counted does not necessarily count; everything that counts cannot necessarily be counted."

If you are a British golfer (Welsh, in Woosnam's case) plying your profession in the birthplace and homeland of a "good walk spoiled," as golf was called by Mark Twain, nothing counts more than winning the Open Championship (known as the British Open on this side of the pond). But a failure to accurately count to fourteen, to comply with one of the few rules in golf that requires a count, can count more than your stroke count in determining whether you can count an Open Championship among your life's achievements.

And so, as the story goes for Woosnam in 2001, everything that can be counted, counted. And in the worst possible way.

Woosnam's career peaked in 1991 when he became the first Welshman to win a major championship by capturing the green jacket at The Masters. That year he rose to No. 1 in the Official World Golf Rankings and would eventually spend fifty weeks on top of the golfing world. But by 2001, a decade following his Masters triumph and four years removed from his last European

Tour win, he was a very different Woosie. He was struggling on the golf course and losing his love of the game. When Woosnam teed off at the British Open that year at Royal Lytham & St. Annes Golf Club, no one had him in the victory pool.

Three days later, when Woosie was back on the tee for the final round and in the final group of the day, tied for the lead, the forty-three-year-old was providing one of the best golfing stories of the year. Could he win? Could he beat a field that included defending champion Tiger Woods and take the Claret Jug?

With a near ace on the 1st hole that turned into a birdie 2 and a final-Sunday lead at the Open, the answer appeared to be yes. But as he teed up his ball at the 2nd and turned to caddie Miles Byrne and asked for his driver, the thoughts of an Open Championship came crashing down around him.

"You're going to go ballistic," said Byrne.

"Why?" asked Woosnam.

"We've got two drivers in the bag."

With thirteen other clubs in the bag and two drivers, that made fifteen. And that is in direct violation of Rule 4-4: *The player shall start a stipulated round with not more than fourteen clubs.* The penalty for said violation is 2 strokes per hole played while the extra club is in tow. And since he'd already played the 1st hole, Woosnam's 1-stroke lead was now a 1-stroke deficit. The unusual fact that Royal Lytham & St. Annes begins with a par-3 1st hole, and thus no one uses a driver, sealed Woosnam's fate. Had Byrne noticed the extra club on the tee to begin the round, it would have been no harm, no foul. Instead, it was the costliest of mistakes.

"At that moment I felt like I'd been kicked in the teeth," Woosnam said.

After angrily throwing his hat and the offending driver, Woosnam bogeyed two of the next three holes. And he admitted later that mentally he couldn't shake the 2-stroke penalty.

"I did not really get it out of my head all the way around. I kept thinking if I hadn't had a two-shot penalty I could have been leading, or been joint leader. I never shook it off."

Woosnam finished with a final round 71, tied for third behind first-time champion David Duval and runner-up Niclas Fasth of Sweden. But the mistake did more than just cost Woosnam his momentum, 2 strokes, a chance at an Open title, and a considerable difference in prize money. If you just gave Woosnam back his 2 lost shots, he would have finished in second place all by himself, instead of in the six-player logjam at third. And that would have resulted in enough Ryder Cup points to move him to sixth in the rankings, instead of twelfth. The top 10 qualify for the Ryder Cup. The rest stay home.

The mistaken club count was Byrne's responsibility, and his alone. But Woosnam was very forgiving, despite everything that the error cost him.

"He's a good caddie. He will have a severe bollocking when I get in, but I am not going to sack him. He's a good lad. It's the biggest mistake he will make in his life and he won't do it again."

Byrne, for his part, also knew where the buck stopped, telling reporters, "You want me to stand here and make excuses. There is no excuse. My fault. Two-shot penalty. End of story."

The end of the story actually came two weeks later at the Scandinavian Masters. Everything was fine between Byrne and Woosnam for the first three rounds. But on the final round Sunday, Byrne overslept and was a no-show for Woosnam's tee time. After breaking into his own locker to retrieve his golf shoes—Byrne had the key—Woosnam was forced to use a local caddie as a stand-in.

When Byrne eventually did surface he was promptly fired by his now much-less-forgiving employer.

"I don't ask for much," said Woosnam. "He had one warning, and that was it."

Culpable Caddie

August 21, 2005—WGC-NEC Invitational Final Round

Professional caddies don't have the on-the-job danger of, say, a demolition industrial diver or Bering Sea crab fisherman. They don't face the same pressures as a pediatric neurosurgeon or NASA's Mission Control flight director. But behind the four-day workweek, loads of frequent-flier miles, snazzy jumpsuits, and an unlimited license to silence the gallery (oh, the power), the life of a caddie can be a cold and lonely place.

Miles Byrne wasn't the only caddie to show up late to work and quickly find himself in the unemployment line. Just six weeks after he was sacked by Ian Woosnam, Byrne's brother Dermot was late to his job holding the bag for Scot Stephen Gallacher at the final round of the European Masters. Someone please introduce this family to the alarm clock.

And sure, the tales of caddie Carl Spackler are legendary. After jumping a ship to Hong Kong and getting on as a caddie at a course in the Tibetan Himalayas, he found himself toting the bag of the Dalai Lama himself. For Spackler's efforts he was granted deathbed total enlightenment, so he's got that going for him.

But like many caddies whose star burns bright, Spackler's time on top was short. He went from caddie of the Lama to golf course assistant groundskeeper all the way down to varmint control. The occasional errant Baby Ruth is now all he has to look forward to.

I am happy to say that caddie Joe Damiano's story differs in many ways from Spackler's. His biography mentions nothing of gophers, explosives, or carrying clubs for a bishop who was struck down by lightning. And not to insult his green thumb, but we are assuming he's never created a hybrid grass out of bluegrass, Kentucky bluegrass, featherbed bent, and northern California sinsemilla (Damon Stoudamire just perked up). Damiano has, however, suffered an on-screen embarrassment in front of millions of people. And he cost his employer, Stuart Appleby, a really, really big paycheck.

Coming down the stretch in the final round of the 2005 WGC-NEC Invitational, and with Appleby in contention, the Australian's 2nd shot on the 13th hole came to a rest on a cart path. Not a problem; Appleby was granted a free drop to gain relief and set up a fairly easy shot to the green.

Appleby routinely dropped the ball. But on a slope, the ball rolled backward, and then caught the cart path again and started to roll away. Reacting quickly, Damiano snatched up the errant drop and handed it back to Appleby so he could have a do-over, as was his right within the rules. But escaping the attention of the two men was the one very big problem with the caddie's fast hands. The ball had not rolled two full club lengths away before Damiano touched it, and that is a big no-no.

Appleby played on, unaware of the infraction. And after a birdie on the 14th hole he found himself just 1 stroke behind the leader, Tiger Woods. But as he walked onto the 15th tee a PGA official was there to break the bad news, and Appleby's spirit, with a 2-stroke penalty. Frustrated, upset, and in a little bit of disbelief, the now-out-of-contention Appleby caved in, posting a double bogey on the 16th and fading down the stretch to finish in a tie for thirteenth place.

Tiger Woods went on to claim the $1.7 million winner's check. Stuart Appleby's share of the prize money ended up being $94,400. And that deficit for Appleby loomed even larger because so many of his endorsement contracts were incentive based. It's estimated that he lost another $1 million (Australian currency) on top of the missed-out prize money. And just in case you're wondering if losing out on that much cash makes you angry, the answer is yes.

"It was a mistake that was very costly," said Appleby. "[Damiano] is a poorer caddie after this week because he won't be getting paid."

He did, however, keep his job.

Kicking a Gift Horse in the Mouth
June 4, 1974—Rangers vs. Indians

As my father-in-law likes to point out, the two most powerful words in the English language, when used consecutively, are "open bar." The potency of those words is so strong that men and women (mostly men) who would otherwise prefer to spend their Saturdays supine on a sofa will instead feel irresistibly drawn to dust off their best suit, put on a tie, and travel several hours and countless miles to attend their least favorite third cousin's long and boring wedding.

One can imagine that if in Homer's *Odyssey* the Sirens had been beckoning Odysseus with the promise of an open bar, instead of merely singing, he might have broken free from the ropes that tied him to his ship's mast and cast himself to the fates of free booze. Of course, because there was no pledge of complimentary cocktails, Odysseus went on to lead every single one of his sailors to their death. So the lesson there: gratis libations save lives.

They also lose baseball games, as Clevelanders learned the hard way in 1974.

In 1973 the Indians averaged just over 7,500 fans a game. In the first two months of the 1974 season those attendance numbers rose modestly to just over 10,000, but in Cleveland's vast 74,400-seat Municipal Stadium that looked like no more than a couple hundred family and friends. It was these Indians, this joke of a franchise, who became the inspiration for the movie *Major League*. These were the laughingstock Indians, a team so bad that the Cuyahoga River's propensity to burst into flames was only the city of Cleveland's second most embarrassing notoriety. The hapless Indians were No. 1.

In 1974 Cleveland was a vast baseball wasteland. Before Jacobs Field, regular sellouts, and appearances in the 1995 and 1997 World Series, they couldn't win, and they most certainly couldn't draw fans.

Until one man with the Indians had a brilliant idea. To loosely quote the world's only talking cornfield: *If you serve it, they will come.*

It was the next best thing to open bar. Cheap beer. And by cheap, we're talking 10 cents a cup cheap. To the surprise of no one who has ever been a beer drinker, known a beer drinker, or seen a beer drinker during the act of drinking, the Indians' cheap beer promotion on June 4, 1974, for a game with the Rangers in town, drew 25,134 "baseball" fans.

Then those fans promptly ruined it for the rest of us by ensuring that no team in its right mind will ever serve really cheap beer again.

The mayhem began at the opening pitch with a series of explosions in the stands. The fans, many of them with plenty of alcohol on board before they arrived at the stadium, had smuggled in firecrackers. By the 2nd inning the rowdiness had escalated into inebriated nudity. A well-fed woman ran onto the field, tried to kiss the umpire, and then bared her breasts to the roar of the beer-goggled throng.

She was a mere warm-up to the show that came in the 4th inning. After the Rangers' Tom Grieve hit his 2nd home run of the game, and while he was still running the bases, a completely naked man ran from the stands and slid into second base. Remember the last time you went camping? And remember even a couple of days after you'd returned home and showered more than once, all of the places where you kept finding dirt? Now imagine doing a full-speed naked dirt slide into second base. How miserable his next week must have been. I say in this case that the punishment fit the crime.

Later in the 4th inning, Rangers manager Billy Martin came onto the field to argue a call, only to be greeted by a shower of beer cups and garbage that would have made Oscar the Grouch jealous. In the 5th a pair of fans ran into the outfield and mooned the bemused Rangers' outfielders, opening the floodgates for the many larger and more brazen groups to follow.

The tidal wave of hooliganism was rising throughout the game. Streakers continued to display their goods. Fans graduated from throwing trash to throwing batteries. And as if Municipal Stadium didn't already have two strikes against it, the fans began to tear up seats and rip up the padding on the outfield walls.

But still they played on. Until the 9th.

The Indians rallied for a pair of runs to knot the game, 5–5, and put the winning run at second base. But the next fan who ran onto the field decided he'd have a little extra fun, so he ran up to Rangers outfielder Jeff Burroughs and knocked Burroughs's hat off his head. Burroughs, reacting to the fan, turned and tripped. And that set off the short-fused Martin in a way never before seen in baseball. Martin grabbed a fungo bat and, with the rest of his team in tow, sprinted to the outfield and to Burroughs's defense.

Burroughs was fine, if perhaps a bit embarrassed by his clumsiness. But the Rangers were far from okay. The fun drunks had been replaced by the angry drunks. And the team's charge into the outfield had sparked outrage among the mob. So, armed with chains, knives, and chunks of stadium, hundreds of fans began to pour out of the stands and onto the field, and a full-blown riot commenced.

Indians manager Ken Aspromonte reacted quickly to the situation, ordering his own players to arm themselves with bats and take the field to help defend the Rangers. Individual skirmishes broke out between fans and players, including current Rangers and future Indians manager Mike Hargrove, who gave a beatdown to a fan who had hit him from behind.

Finally the players and umpires escaped the field and crew chief Nestor Chylak ruled the result was a Cleveland forfeit. But not before Chylak was hit in the head by a tossed chair while watching a thrown hunting knife stick blade down in the grass just inches from his leg. His postgame analysis was this: "F——animals!"

The police finally made it to the stadium with numbers strong enough to disperse the crowd. But even then, it took another thirty minutes for Cleveland's finest to clear the field of the last of Cleveland's lowest. Nine arrests were made.

Indians management bears much of the responsibility for cheap beer night gone wrong. They didn't employ any extra security that night and they allowed each fan to purchase up to six beers at a time, with no restrictions on how many times they could return for more. When the transfer of beer from Stroh's truck to concession stand failed to keep up with the fans' demand, the team allowed the drinkers to go directly to the trucks lined up beyond the outfield fence and get refills there.

So yes, the team is significantly at fault for the remaining three promotions that they had planned for the rest of the season getting canceled by AL president Lee McPhail. But the true villains in all of this, the people who will forever carry the stink of the scorn of the masses for taking a good thing—no, a *great* thing—and completely blowing it, are the fans.

Your neighbor, with the incredible pool, giant plasma TV, and NFL Sunday Ticket just asked you to house-sit for six months. But you decided it would be more fun to piss him off by toilet-papering his house.

You, Cleveland Indian fans, should be ashamed. Even Stroh's is too good for you.

Steve Bartman
October 14, 2003—NL Championship Series Game 6, Marlins vs. Cubs

Marge, don't discourage the boy! Weaseling out of things is important to learn. It's what separates us from the animals! Except the weasel.
—Homer Simpson

A half dozen or so fans reached for the 8th-inning foul ball that started the string of falling dominoes that changed the outcome of Game 6 of the 2003 NLCS. But it was Steve Bartman who got his hand on it, immediately ending his life as an anonymous Cubs fan. (© *John Zich/NewSport/Corbis*)

It was perhaps, at least in my estimation, the worst case of weaseling out in sports history. The cursed Cubs, destined to live in the world of Major League Baseball as "lovable losers," added another season's graceless exit to their long history by blowing a 3-run lead to the Marlins in Game 6 of the 2003 National League Championship Series. They were just five outs away from playing in their first World Series since 1945. You have to go back to 1908 to find the last time the Cubs won the World Series.

But instead of acknowledging that sometimes the baseball doesn't bounce your way, and instead of blaming the pitchers, fielders, and hitters who let the lead slip away and then went out and lost the following night in Game 7, history tells us that the fault for the Cubs' collapse lies with a bespectacled twenty-six-year-old Little League coach named Steve Bartman.

Oh sure, Bartman looks innocent enough. He appears to be the kind of guy that you'd want to date your daughter, do your taxes, house-sit your dogs, or, ironically, coach your son's Little League team. But don't be fooled by his friendly face and pleasant demeanor. This "Joe Everyman" is a baseball dream killer. It was Bartman who intentionally and maliciously interfered with left fielder Moises Alou, preventing him from retiring Luis Castillo on a pop fly foul ball, and single-handedly robbing the Cubs of their best chance to win a World Series in ninety-five years. He kicked your dog, told your kids there was no Santa Claus, and insulted your mother, all in one single act. Why isn't he in Guantánamo?

Of course, this version of the history texts assumes that the reader is either (a) completely insane, or (b) a complete idiot.

First and foremost, all Steve Bartman did was try and catch a foul ball. It's the dream of every baseball fan to catch a batted ball. It's why kids, both young and old, bring their gloves to the stadium each night. And then to catch one in what was arguably the most important game for the Cubs in nearly six decades makes it a dream almost too good to be realized. Bartman was living his dream, our dream. He did the very thing that every single one of us would have done had we been lucky enough to hold his ticket that night. And for that, he was persecuted.

Then there are the events that occurred A.B. (after Bartman). Keep in mind that no runs were scored, no one reached base safely, and no one moved into scoring position because of Steve Bartman.

It was Mark Prior who walked Castillo, throwing the wild pitch that moved Juan Pierre to third. It was Mark Prior who then gave up a run-scoring single to Ivan Rodriguez. It was Alex S. Gonzalez who booted Miguel Cabrera's potential inning-ending double-play ball, keeping the Marlins alive. It was Mark Prior, again, who gave up the 2-run game-tying double to Derrek Lee. It was manager Dusty Baker who called on his bullpen to intentionally walk not one but two Marlins. And it was Kyle Farnsworth who gave up a sacrifice fly between those intentional walks and then a bases-clearing double by Mike Mordecai to make the score 7–3, Florida. A Juan Pierre single made it 8–3 before the inning finally came to a close when Castillo, the man who started it all, popped out to second.

The inning featured 12 batters, 5 hits, 3 walks, an error, 8 runs scored, and 43 pitches thrown. But not one of those pitches was made by Steve Bartman.

The next night, in Game 7, the Cubs led 5–3 heading into the 5th. In that inning they gave up 2 hits, 2 walks, and 3 runs on 22 pitches. Again, not a single pitch was thrown by Steve Bartman. He also didn't bat, not even one time, as the Cubs ended their season by failing to mount a Game 7 comeback.

The *Cubs* lost Game 6 and Game 7 all by themselves. Yet thanks to angry and delusional fans, idiots on talk radio, the nimrods who made a public spectacle of exploding the Bartman ball, and *Chicago Sun-Times* columnist Jay Mariotti, who wrote, "A fan in that situation should try his best to get out of the way, even if he isn't of the mind to see Alou approaching, as Bartman claims" (as if Bartman was lying), the myth of Bartman's guilt gained legs and the Cubs were allowed to weasel out of their own culpability.

Mark Prior did take responsibility for his part in the meltdown, telling reporters, "I hung an 0-2 curveball to Rodriguez. Everybody in this clubhouse knows [the Bartman] play was not the reason we lost."

But Prior's words were virtually ignored by the Chicago fans and media.

When almost five year later, in April 2008, Alou told the Associated Press, "You know what the funny thing is? I wouldn't have caught [the ball] anyway," the Chicago press was again absent, barely finding room in a buried back-page paragraph for Alou's exoneration.

Maybe Alou finds his inability to catch the ball ironic humor, but it's not so funny to Bartman, who endured the kind of threats and harassment usually reserved for baby killers and tax collectors. It would have been nice of Alou to not wait five years to clear Bartman of blame.

It is time to declare that Steve Bartman's place in baseball history is as a Cubs fan and nothing more. He's not a goat; he's not part of a curse; and he was not a factor in the 2003 NLCS. Bartman just happened to be in the wrong place at the wrong time, and his actions that night deserved nothing more than a Homer Simpson "D'oh!"

For the weasels who've blamed Bartman since that October night in 2003, please always remember this Homer Simpsonism: "When you participate in sporting events, it's not whether you win or lose; it's how drunk you get."

ABOUT THE AUTHOR

Kyle Garlett is a freelance sportswriter who has written for *ESPN: The Magazine*, FoxSports.com, and a variety of programs on Fox Sports Net, including *The Best Damn Sports Show Period* and *The Ultimate Fantasy Football Show*. He lives in Marina del Rey, California.